Pedra Parada · S.ta Olaia · **Lousa** · S. Antão do Tojal · T

Amarge do Bispo · Alvogas Velhas · A. dos Moninhos · A. dos Borreiros · A. dos Vaos · Tojalinho · Pinheiro · Lagariça · Q.ta do Bom Successo · Sette Casas · Ponte de Lousa · R. de Lousa · Salanes

Machado · M.te da Sardinha · A. dos Calvos · Barro · **Loures** · Mealhada · S.to Antonio dos Capuchos · **Friell**

Ouril · Corvão · Apeizão · Q.ta do Marchão · Pont de Friellas · **Appell**

S.ra dos Enfermos · S.ta Trindade do Sabugo

Sabugo · Canessas · D.na Maria · Povoa de S. Adrião

Monte Gordo · Camara · Trigaxe · **Odivellas** · **Charneca**

Agualva · Venda Seca · S. Mamede · Fonte Santa · Agua livre · A. da Beja

Carapinheque · Carenque · Aqueduc · Mira · Abobara · Pombaes · Castello · **Amexoeira**

Indenha · **Bellas** · Carenque · Chã · Felgueira · **Lumiar** · **Campo Grande**

Q.ta de S. Mera · Vintra · **Porcalhota** · Paço de Lumiar · Telheiras · Entre campos · Campo pequeno

QUELUS · Fontaine · Aqueduc · **Carnide** · Luz · Rego · Arco do

his de Baixo · **Bemfica** · Palma de Cima

da Serra · S.to Antonio da Tercena · d'Agua · Calhari

F.ca da Polvera · Cazal da Serra · Viteiro · S. Domingos de Bemfica · Pallavam · S. Sebastião da Pedreira · Nel

Barcarena · Linhá Pastora · Alfragides · Portela · Monsanto · Arroios · Penha de F

R. de · **Carnaxide** · Quejas

Murganhol · Linhá a Velha · Outurela · Q.ta do Prior · **LISBONNE** · Campo d'Ourig

aveiras · Q.ta do Merel · Cazelas · Penedo

Caxias · S.ta Catharina · F. de S. Joze · N.a S.a d'Ajuda · Arseal de la Ma

F. de S. Bruno · Boa Viagem · Argeis · Alcolena · Junqueira · Alcantara

Aros · da Boa Viagem · Jose de Ribamar · S.ta Cruz Quebrada · F. da Arca · F. da Conceição · **BELEM** · Bom Successo · **PORT DE LISBONNE** · Cassilha

de Paço de Arcos · T. de Belem

SINTRA

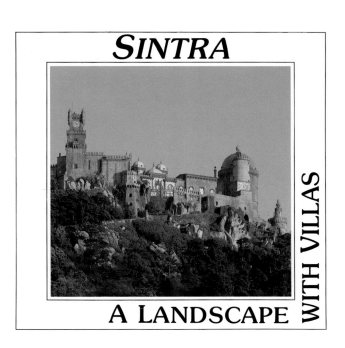

A LANDSCAPE WITH VILLAS

JOSÉ CORNÉLIO DA SILVA • GERALD LUCKHURST

PHOTOGRAPHY BY ANTÓNIO HOMEM CARDOSO

SINTRA

A LANDSCAPE WITH VILLAS

EDIÇÕES
inapa

The Genius of the Place Collection

Photography by
António Homem Cardoso

Design by
Ana Filipa Amaral Neto Tainha

The watercolour on pages 10, 11 e 15
are by the father of the author
José Cornélio da Silva

and those on pages 25 and 45 are by
Fernando Perfeito de Magalhães

© Texts — José Cornélio da Silva, 1989
© Edições Inapa, 1989
Translation by Anne Ridd
Photocomposition by
Textype, Artes Gráficas, Lda.
Proof-reading by Maria José Mascarenhas
Colour-separation by Reproscan,
Reprodução Gráfica, Lda.
Printing by Printer Portuguesa,
Indústria Gráfica, Lda.
Legal Deposit No. 107 316/97
ISBN 972-8387-21-0

Index

INTRODUCTION

Sintra has recently attracted a growing interest, as demonstrated by various publications that dedicate themselves to its many and varied delights. It should be remembered however that *Sintra* is a whole district with a special personality and an architectural and natural character very much of its own.

It was with this motivation that we have examined the historic and artistic phenomenon that is *Sintra* in all its varied facets: climatic, botanical, colourful, architectural, social and literary conditions that have over the course of time created a wonderful piece of landscape. We have sought to divulge the mentality and the philosophy that is known of those who live in the *Villas of Sintra*, and people who meet and take long walks in the mountains, or even those who know the true call of Art and Nature.

We have tried to make clear this love for *Sintra* and to illuminate some of its historical byways. In this way, not of travel literature, but rather as a modest cicerone, we offer to share our passion and enthusiasm for the *Serra*.

If the chapters of the book separate the various moments of life in *Sintra* that ought to be juxtapositioned then this is simply a question of method for the historic message of *Sintra* is just this: a result of continuity and permanence.

The authors wish to recognize the collaboration and ready cooperation of Luís Mergulhão and Vítor Serrão in the making of this work.

For assistance with our investigations, we wish to thank the Town Library of Sintra, the Gulbenkian Foundation, the National Library in Lisbon, the Library of the Academia de Bellas Artes and the British Historical Society, Lisbon.

Thanks should also be made to all those who made detailed contributions towards the conclusion of the book, especially Regina Anacleto, José Manuel Carneiro, Sérgio Luís Carvalho, Rachel Cook, the late Francisco Costa, Alexander Hamilton-Fletcher, João Almeida Flor, Salvatore Gentile, Richard Kingsbury, Priscilla Metcalf, José Cardim Ribeiro, Hermínio Santos, Judith Swaddling and Christopher Thacker.

Clearly such a book could not have been written without the collaboration and participation of the owners of the properties visited, by whom we were greeted with charming sympathy. Albeit that some quintas have passed from family ownership to corporate entities, the hospitality received from each rapidly led us to forget this difference.

Jersey (Channel Islands)

Monserrate! The very thought of it takes me back to 1946 when I first met Francis, my late husband — I sat next to him at a dinner party and most of the conversation was of Monserrate, his great love for the place, his description of the parties in the thirties, leaving from Tilbury Docks by ship, stories of the joyful games on board and of a special cabin always reserved for the Stilton cheese which the family could not possibly do without for six weeks. On arrival being met by the Agent, Mr. Oram, the processional drive to Monserrate; on his very first visit at the age of four this must have been exciting to a degree — on arrival at the Palace being met by Julio the Butler and Maria the Housekeeper, but most of all his happy memories were of the garden, a wonderful and unique garden where he spent many hours writing poetry, painting and just drinking in the beauty and magnificence of the place.

On the few occasions that I have been to Monserrate I felt that I too had lived there from time to time, so vivid were my memories of the house and garden as told to me by Francis. I find an affinity for Monserrate and the Portuguese people just as Francis has said in the past, and especially the lovely feeling of peace and tranquility that one finds in this magical garden. Because of this I am glad to learn that the beautiful garden which was so carefully planned and lovingly cared for by my late husband's family may once again be planned and cared for by a new generation, and I wish the project every success.

Brenda Lady Cook
Viscondessa de Monserrate

THE NATURAL LANDSCAPE OF SINTRA

INTRA is a lovely spot, in fact «perhaps in every respect the most delightful in Europe, it contains beauties of every description natural and artificial. Palaces and gardens rising in the midst of rocks, cataracts and precipices; convents on stupendous heights, a distant view of the Tagus... it unites in itself all the wildness of the Western Highlands with the verdure of the South of France.»[1]

Approached from Cascais on the long winding and always climbing road, with the sea far below and windmills on the hilltops, the district of Sintra introduces itself abruptly. Best make the journey in the evening, watch the sun setting on the ocean, feel the cool breezes rushing towards your destination.

The landscape around Cascais is arid: a low spikey heathland of gorse. Here and there small houses huddle in deep valleys — out of the wind that drove all those mills. This landscape repeats itself monotonously, made exciting only by the sharp bends in the road and the sheer drops to the sea below. *In an instant* everything changes, crossing the ridge the road begins to descend and laid out before you is the verdant prospect of the fertile valley of Colares. The wind still blows here, many of the vineyards around you are protected behind screens of giant reeds, but down in the valley are orchards of all kinds, neat vegetable gardens and running brooks: an Arcadian scene.

The evening breezes bring with them a light mist cooling and easing the heat of the day. The traveller from Lisbon or Cascais is soothed; the fruits of the valley are refreshed.

Continuing now past the village of Colares you begin to notice, between gaps in the overhanging trees «palaces and gardens in the midst of rocks»[2], these are the «Quintas of Sintra»[3], and, to your right now, the mountain range you have crossed: the Serra de Sintra. Byron saw the Serra before the great re-planting of the mountain was initiated by King Fernando II in the mid-nineteenth century — today these palaces are surrounded by the magnificent forests of that Romantic vision. But these views are fast closing, those mists are mingling with the vapours above and as you rise again into the village of Sintra you find yourself literally in the clouds: you will have to wait

View of the Serra de Sintra, from Janas.

View of the Serra de Sintra from Janas (watercolour by the father of the author, José Cornélio da Silva).

View of the road to Pena.

til morning for those «convents on stupendous heights». To make this trip is to fall in love with Sintra, the best possible introduction.

It is in vain that I call upon clouds to cover me and fogs to wrap me up. You can form no adequate idea of the continual glare of this renowned climate. Lisbon is the place in the world best calculated to make me cry out 'Hide me from the day's garish eye'. But where to hide is not so easy. [4]

I must go to Sintra or I shall expire! [5]

William Beckford writing from Lisbon in May expresses a desire to be found in every travel-book. «Cool, heavenly cool Cintra», said Southey. [6] Because of fogs, mists and clouds borne on sea breezes Sintra enjoys the cool temperate summers of the north: it is in this aspect that the town contrasts most strongly with its surroundings. Modern tourists from Lisbon are surprised in their T-shirts and shorts, conspicuous amongst the woolly-jumpered residents.

Sintra has long been recognized as a remarkable phenomenon in the climatic atlas of Portugal, but its unique position in relation to the Atlantic and Mediterranean influences make it remarkable in Europe. This is particularly so when considered in relation to the growth of the plants.

Such is the power of the climate, that the gardenias and Cape plants that I brought with me from England, mere stumps, are covered with beautiful blossoms. The curled mallows, and some varieties of Indian-corn, sown by my English gardener, have shot up to a strange elevation, and begin to form shady avenues and fairy forests, where children might play in perfection at landscape-gardening. [7]

Beckford noticed this extraordinary power of the climate within six weeks of his arrival in Portugal.

Sintra is such a garden. Byron called Sintra a «Glorious Eden» and has been quoted thoughtlessly ever since, but Southey called it «my Paradise» before and Gil Vicente in 1529, «um jardim do paraíso terreal». They all knew their Genesis:

And the Lord planted a garden in Eden, in the East;
and there he put man whom he had formed.
And out of the ground the Lord God made to grow
every tree that is pleasant to the sight and
good for food... [8]

THE SERRA

For travellers to Portugal the Serra de Sintra was the important landmark announcing their arrival in Lisbon and promising future resort.

We saw Berlengs last night. This morning I rose at five. We were off the Rock, the Sun seemed to rest their as he rose behind it, the tower of Mafra visible. As we advanced the heights of Cintra arose and the Pena Convent. [9]

The rocky mountain character of the Serra de Sintra was very appealing to the Romantic travellers even those who set out to descry rather than declaim:

The sounds and prospects peculiar to it are very favourable to reflection, particularly of a stormy day, where the murmurs of surges and the howling of tempests fill the mind with a sympathetic sadness. Wherever we turn our eyes, the mind is struck with the awful works of Nature: on one side is the distant ocean whose surface blends with the blue horizon; beneath the deep valley strikes one with the appearance of an august cavern; the shattered state of impending rock on the declivity of the mountain, torn as it were asunder, and everywhere bursting from the soil, threaten at the least shock to tumble down and destroy the village. [10]

But this awful aspect is contrasted with the luxuriance of the vegetation «It unites in itself all the wildness of the Western Highlands with the verdure of the South of France» [11] — and it is this conjunction that has appealed to travellers of all times.

The mossy fragments of rock, grotesque pollards and rustic bridges you meet at every step recall Savoy or Switzerland to the imagination; but the exotic cast of the vegetation, the vivid green of the citron, the golden fruitage of the orange, the blossoming myrtle, and the rich fragrance of the turf, embroidered with the brightest coloured and the most aromatic flowers, allow me without a violent stretch of fancy to believe my self in the garden of Hesperides, and expect the dragon under every tree. [12]

North and South combined!

The vegetation of the Serra de Sintra is described with the same attention. Southey devotes a letter [13] to a description of his three favourite trees:

View of the Serra de Sintra (watercolour by José Cornélio da Silva).

The cork is perhaps the most beautiful of trees: its leaves are small, and have the dusky colour of evergreens, but its boughs branch out in the most fantastic twisting of the oak, and its bark is of all others the most picturesque; — you have seen deal curl under the carpenter's plane — it grows in such curls, — the wrinkles are of course deep, one might fancy the cavities the cells of the hermit fairies. There is one tree in particular here which a painter might well come from England to see, large and old; its trunk and branches are covered with fern — the yellow sunburnt fern — forming so sunny a contrast to the dark foliage! — a wild vine winds up and hangs in festoons from the boughs, its leaves of a bright green, like youth, — and now the purple clusters are ripe…

The chestnut is also beautiful; its blossoms shoot out in rays like stars, and now its hedgehog fruit stars the dark leaves.

The Fir; — not such as you have seen, but the one that shoots out no branches, grows very high, and then spreads broad in a mushroom shape exactly — the bottom of its head the brown and withered colour that the yew and the fir always have and the surface of the brightest green — you might consider a giant picking one of these pines for a parasol — they have something of the appearance in the distance that the palm and the cocoa has in a print.

But rather than individual trees it is the profusion and variety of plant growth that delights — amongst the rocks — the twisted boughs and ferny, mossy coverings that impress. Combined with rushing brooks and gushing fountains this is the image of the Serra.

THE PLANALTO

Between the Serra de Sintra and Mafra to the north lies the high plateau — the remains of the marine platform of limestone — known as the Planalto. It is here that the best marble is found. It is, by comparison to Sintra, an inhospitable place, in the full blasts of the northern winds. Beckford made a trip to Mafra, across this plain, in August:

We got into the carriage at nine, in spite of the wind, which blew full in our faces. The distance from the villa I inhabit (Ramalhão) to this stupendous convent is about fourteen English miles, and the road, which by good luck has been lately mended, conducted across a parched open country, thinly scattered with windmills and villages. The retrospect on the woody slopes

Planalto to the north of Sintra, Odrinhas.

The Serra at Penedo.

and pointed rocks of Cintra is pleasant enough, but when you look forward nothing can be more bleak or barren than the prospect. [14]

THE LITORAL

The litoral «is truly picturesque, and consists of bold projections, intermixed with pyramidal rocks succeeding each other in theatrical perspective, the most distinct crowned by a lofty tower, which serves as a lighthouse. No words can convey an adequate idea of the bloom of the atmosphere, and the silvery light reflected from the sea. From the edge of the abyss, where I had remained several minutes like one spellbound, we descended a winding path, about half a mile, to the beach. Here we found ourselves nearly shut in by shattered cliffs and grottos, a fantastic amphitheatre, the best calculated that can be possibly imagined to invite the sports of sea nymphs. Such coves, such deep and broken recesses, such a play of outline I never beheld, nor did I ever hear so powerful a roar of rushing waters on any other coast». [15] No words can convey an adequate idea: go there like Camões to Cabo da Roca or Beckford to Praia da Adraga and behold for yourself.

THE CHARNECA

Refering to the Charneca, as late as 1930 an American guidebook to Portugal recommends that visitors to Sintra should take the train «for the road is very poor and dusty». Eça de Queirós in *The Maias* (1888) describes the journey [16] of Carlos and Cruges:

After a while they entered the Charneca, which seemed to them interminable. On both sides, as far as the eye could see, was a dark and sad land, and above an endless blue, which in that solitude seemed sad also. The regular trot of the horses bore monotonously on the road, yet there was not a stir save occasionally a bird that cut through the air with an abrupt flight, fleeing from the rough wilderness.

THE VARZEA

Of the Várzea, Beckford wrote:

I thought myself entering the orchards of Alcinous. The boughs literally bent under the fruit; the slightest shake strewed the ground with plums, oranges and apricots... I never saw plants more conspicuous for size and vigor than these which have the luck of being sown in this fortunate soil. [17]

The litoral, Guincho.

From these descriptions it will be appreciated that Sintra, as a district with a special intrinsic environmental conditions, is limited to the Litoral, The Varzea, and quintessentially, to the Serra — here we find the «temperate mediterranean maritime climate» and it is here that we find especially favoured microclimates. The plains of the Charneca and the Planalto are as the sea to an island or perhaps the desert to an oasis, by contrast making Sintra all the more «remarkably damp».

«It would be possible to wander for days», wrote Sacheverall Sitwell «in this damp and foggy Sintra which seems alone and isolated in a curious way, as though it is an Atlantic Island put down on the mainland».[18] The plains serve to isolate Sintra giving it a magical quality that has been the appeal of Sintra from the earliest times. It is perhaps easiest to appreciate the Landscape of Sintra from this point of view.

Byron's «Glorious Eden»[19]. Beckford always more classically-minded called it Elysian — both were places apart from the world, resorts in the true sense of the word. But these are concepts of the human mind, the natural environment of Sintra, and thus the basis for all that Man has built there is best described by Eça de Queirós: «a little bit of Moss...»[20]

Facing page,
Praia da Ursa (the Bear's Beach), Roca.
Right, *view of the Serra de Sintra*
from the south
Below, *view of Praia das Maçãs (Apple Beach),*
Praia Grande (The Great Beach)
and Roca (The Rock of Lisbon)
(Watercolour by José Cornélio da Silva).

ANCIENT SETTLEMENTS OF THE SINTRA REGION

F ROM the end of the Bronze Age and the beginning of the Iron Age to the sixth and the seventh centuries, family farming units were concentrated on volcanic land this provided easier farming. These ancient rural traditions continue to promote the area and have given rise to intensive settlement throughout History. Archaelogical remains have been found in Sintra, wich gives us an idea of the strong trade links that existed between its original inhabitants and the sea-faring people of North Africa such as the Carthaginians, as well as the civilizations of the Eastern Mediterranean, and particularly the Phoenicians. Olissipo, the Roman city of Lisbon, lying on the Tagus Estuary, possessed however, superior opportunities and became the centre for trade. At the same time therefore the Sintra region began to specialise in farming. This was a successful development for both entities, which in its turn created an interdependence that, despite changing circumstances, continues today.

These established commercial links brought about a Roman-like form of social organization. Dealings with large Mediterranean ports caused the import of Roman uses and practises, not to mention customs, which went a long way towards facilitating the sort of «official Romanization» attributed to the period when Olissipo was fortified by the Legion of Decimus Iunius Brutus in 138 B. C.

There were many Roman *Villae* in the Lisbon area, distributed on the «planalto» to the North of Sintra. They were formed by large farms with areas ranging from 900 to 1200 hectares which constituted the mainstay and affluence of the municipal elite of Lisbon. These rich landowners governed Olissipo from the luxurious *triclinium* of these opulent *villae*, surrounded by rich architecture, monuments, engraved stones, altars and geometric pavings of multicoloured *tesselae*. The Roman *villae* of São Marcos, close to Cacém, of Santo André in Almoçageme, and São Miguel, in Odrinhas, are typical examples of this type settlement or land-based wealth.

The agricultural development of the «planalto» supported a considerable population. It is supposed from the size, prosperity and density of Roman remains and monuments found in the zone that a city once existed. Finds have included baths and sporting grounds.

Roman Mosaic
São Miguel de Odrinhas.

Oecus, Roman Villa at São Miguel de Odrinhas.

Roman exploration of the land was not limited to extensive agriculture; marble (still a great source of wealth in the region) and metallic ores (namely the «carbuncles» of Pliny the Elder that he mentions at the «Suimo mines») were extracted.

By the end of the third and fourth centuries the decadence of the Roman Empire and the permanent pressure exerted by the barbarian incursions were also beginning to be felt in the Sintra area.

This would explain the ascent of the various populations up to the «serra» of Sintra; they preferred the hills to the «planalto» which was vulnerable and difficult to defend by the weary and disorganized minorities, bereft of their murdered leaders. The «serra» of Sintra which had attained the designation of Mons Sacro was regarded as a propitious and natural bastion of defence, and so late Roman settlements began to appear on the hillside (circa 5th century), around the nucleus which was later to become the town of Sintra.

The Visigoths continued to occupy the Roman sites adapting them for their own needs. Curiously there seem to have been some adaptations made on these villae, of greater architectural quality, such as São Miguel de Odrinhas, which became a Christian temple.

The arrival in Spain of Muca Ibne Nocair in 712 established a new order, repercussions of which were deeply felt until the reign of King Manuel (1495-1521) when the Muslims were absorbed. The Muslims were responsible for the fixed settlement of the great urban and market centres which they fortified and improved. They also recovered the art of gardening, lost since the Roman times.

According to written records of this period, Sintra continued to be of significance during the Muslim domination, it was one of the three chief towns of the Muslim... «province of Balata, where are Santarém, Lisbon and Sintra».[21]

A text by Ahmede Arrazi contains important information for us since it refers to Sintra by not only stressing its regional and provincial importance, but also mentioning the existence of «two castles». As these observations can be dated to the 10th century, it is easy to conclude that they refer to the Moorish castle on top of the mountain (an essentially military structure); and the lower Palace of the Moorish walis with its Alcazar and encircling walls.

The Muslim origins of the present Sintra National Palace have been definitely proved by several authors, such as Borges Coelho

Visigothic tombs built over the ruins of the Roman Villa at São Miguel de Odrinhas.

*The Moorish Castle.
Facing page, below,
the Museum of Roman Epigraphy.*

and Francisco Costa. Muslim heritage has given Sintra lasting models, in the same way that the Roman heritage has lived on through the Italian Renaissance. As a consequence of Moorish investment in the area: building techniques, the introduction of exotic botanical species from other lands wich adapted well to its diversified microclimates; the region became heavily populated. This is turn led to increased building. Two contemporary descriptions of the Moorish province of Andaluz give us an idea of Sintra at this time:

The Andaluz has been compared by many authors to Paradise on earth... as it is well known that perpetual Paradise is that in which the acorn, the hazelnut, the walnut, the chestnut and other fruits of Northern climes grow together with bananas, sugar cane and other products from hot climates... When I spoke of giving a just and suitable description of the Andaluz, I meant to say that it is a country surrounded by the sea, with abundant fruits and crops of all kinds, with many towns and villages inhabited to such an extent that if a traveller were to travel a certain distance he would at every step find villages, towns, rustic villas and cultivated fields and will never see, as it is the case of many other countries, large areas of land which are uncultivated or deserted. This is also linked to the habits of the Andalucians who, instead of living together, grouped into towns as do the Egyptians, preferring to reside in small houses and dwellings in the middle of fields, by the side of streams and on the slopes of hills, which gives the country an air of comfort and prosperity which the traveller will seek in vain in other countries. Besides, it is a pleasure to see their houses, which are constantly whitewashed, inside and out, contrasted with the green of the trees; and, in the words of the famous Vizir and poet Ibne Alhimara, in his description of Andaluz «Its villages shine among the trees like unmatched pearls, encrusted in a sea of emeralds. [22]

Where else could we find finer and more historic words to describe, in such an impressive and almost «modern» fashion, the typical settlement of which this region is an example? Thus «we have the *almuinhas* (from the Arab almunya, meaning a wall-enclosed farm), which are *quintas* close to rivers or streams.

These *almuinhas* become more numerous on the Peninsula from the eleventh century onwards and correspond almost exactly to the basic ideals of all the Hispano-Arabs: that is, to possess this kind of property (of obvious Muslim origins), surrounded by gardens interspersed with fruit trees. [23]

That the Muslim occupation had become an almost natural state of affairs, is even recognized in the very text of the Town Charter for Sintra (1154), where the muslims represented a sizeable part of the population.

All these signs lead us to conclude that there is much which remains of Muslim origin in the culture of the region.

The initial phase of settlement had come to an end, the rural area was defined and the importance of the Town of Sintra stressed; only after the Christian conquest of the Moors in the twelfth century and particularly from the reign of King John I, with the new restructuring of the Portuguese State at the end of the 14th century, will the idea of a settlement spreading out from the centre of the town take hold again.

SINTRA AROUND THE ROYAL PALACE

THE successful re-conquest of Santarém[24] from the Moors by the armies of King Afonso (d. 1185) greatly encouraged the undertaking of the conquest of Lisbon. This he achieved on 25 October 1147, aided by foreign military forces consisting of the armies of Louis VII of France and Conrad III, first Hohenstaufen Emperor, who joined King Afonso on their way to the II Crusade. A few weeks later, in November, Sintra, the third important city of the province Balata, surrendered and the celestial cross of the Christians was hoisted at the Castle.

In Sintra the transfer of power was accomplished without a struggle, safeguarding the population, economic interests and buildings. Referring, however, to housing and building we should mention the further occupation and transformation of places already in existence and the later erection of Christian churches, at first on the outskirts and then in the centre of the town of Sintra, around which the medieval houses developed.

It was the Charter of 9th January 1154, signed by King Afonso, Queen Mafalda and Chancellor Alberto, which consecrated the rights of the people and brought the town of Sintra officially and administratively back into the recently formed Kingdom. This same document is a valuable source of information on the layout of Christian settlement in the town of Sintra. From the *castellum* (representing the military fortification and not the *Alcazar*) the abode of 30 settlers to whom the Charter was granted, housing began to spread towards the town with progressive building on the hillside. Here the church of São Miguel was built. The document also granted independence as regards taxes and local government; and gave the community and the municipal organization the right to appoint the highest authority of the district and his assistant. The relatively fast development of Sintra was due, no doubt, to the special benefits granted to its inhabitants. This applied both to the tribute paying class of «menores» (merchants, artisans, Jews and Moors) and to those who paid no tribute, called «maiores». As Francisco Costa aptly observed, apart from a considerable tax on wheat, barley and wine levied on the *menores,* from the time of the 1154 Charter to the reign of King Manuel (1495-1521), no-one paid

Royal Palace of Sintra.

The Manueline Charter of Sintra.

taxes in the municipality of Sintra. By the end of King Afonso's reign (1185), the town of Sintra had more or less achieved the layout and extension of the so-called Vila-Velha of today, with houses around the Churches of São Miguel, São Pedro, Santa Maria and São Martinho.

Agriculturally, the former structure was maintained until the beginning of the 14th century; by that time the Muslim threat had been definitely set aside and the consequent stability felt by the people led them to descend to the plains. They formed small-holdings, employing hired men and freed Moors, who made up the local work force.

It is obvious that the administration under King Afonso gave an important stimulus to the development of Sintra during the first dynasty.

Aside from these economic interests, we know that the Portuguese Kings came to Sintra for hunting, particularly falconry which was already famous during the Moorish occupation. In fact, game was so abundant that the people of Sintra brought it to the attention of the Royal Courts. It was therefore necessary to adapt the former Moorish Alcazar for the Christian Court.

Though the planning was Christian, as certainly were the master craftsmen, there is no doubt that the labourers were Moors, as is confirmed by the following quotation from a Royal Charter dated 1281. King Dinis (reigned 1279-1325) carried out works of:

Renovation and Restoration to the existing palace at Oliva, in the centre of the old town, as distinct from the Castle itself built at the top of the hill, whose old houses of the *almedinas* and towers would be preserved by the freed moors of Colares. On a par with the Christians, these moors only paid one-quarter and not one-half of the fruit picked, on conditions of rendering that service, called «anuduva or renovation of castles». [25]

This seems to be the missing explanation for the architectural interpretation of the Palace of Sintra set down here in a document: the Moorish tradition of the building was due not only to its Moorish foundation but also to the fact that the Moors continued to maintain it until the Manueline period. This permanent influence of the freed

*Engravings taken from the «Book of Fortresses»,
by Duarte D'Armas, showing the Royal Palace.*

Moors of Colares in all successive restorations of the palace would have preserved its Moorish architectural character: unity was maintained owing to the fact that both the construction techniques and the labourers were Moorish. Christian intervention consisted in individual additions only such as the gothic windows of the Royal Chapel, and some doors and windows.

It is likely that the alterations at the palace served as model for other, mainly civil, constructions. As regards the churches however, both the models and the types of construction are Christian, as is the case of the above-mentioned churches of São Miguel, Santa Maria, São Pedro e São Martinho (in its original form). The typical ogival apertures, essentially Christian, point to the «new architecture».

Thus the first dynasty sees Sintra becoming organized and administratively integrated into the Kingdom, and visited several times by the Royal family who began to appreciate it for its merits as a pleasant and healthy area. However it is in the reign of John I (1385-1433), founder of the II dynasty [26], that the Court began to spend long periods at the Sintra Palace.

The three drawings by Duarte d'Armas reproduced here are an architectural landmark *par excellence*: they point out on the one hand the special interest of the Portuguese Kings in Sintra by their having a large residence where all the Court could be housed and, on the other, a profusion of architectural elements which mark the beginning of a new language. It is not a castle that we see, but rather a nucleus of buildings, bristling on one side with towers, which although fortified at the level of the first and second floors, are pierced by large double windows on the exterior. It is in these elements and in the lower buildings and doors in rusticated style, not to mention the semicircular windows (since some of the ogival windows appear to have been altered, perhaps to give them a more «Roman» look), that we can see the birth of the new mentality: King Manuel (reigned 1495-1521) was to introduce late gothic, so-called Manueline, and classicist architecture to the palace; the Italian Renaissance influence from the reign of King John III (1521-1557) onwards forced the higher levels of society to concern themselves with artistic values, particularly architecture, and encouraged a new attitude to the landscape.

St. Mary's Church, Sintra.

The Manueline Wing of the Royal Palace.

The fountain found today in the Jardim da Preta (Garden of the Negress) at the Royal Palace of Sintra (watercolour by Fernando Perfeito de Magalhães).

Sintra

THE *VILLA RUSTICA* AND *THE VILLA URBANA*

E-ANIMATED from the fifteenth century onwards by the constant presence of the Court in its royal palaces and the rising aristocracy who established town and country seats and also wealth producing bourgeoisie who all encouraged artistic activities and building, the town of Sintra during the first half of the 16th century lived a period of splendour.[27]

Sintra possessed the ideal setting for the Renaissance court with a luxuriant mountain range, watered by countless streams (some of the freshest in the country according to Duarte Nunes do Leão), and an almost mythological vegetation and scenery containing many animals. The ever-changing landscape lent itself to fantastic musings which, from the *subtegmine fagi*[28] to the concealed caverns, were evocative of the writing of Plato and Aristotle or, as legendary as the myths of the nymphs and muses, extending to the tritons who emerged from the waves to appease the sea: a true paradise of nymphs, wood-nymphs and naiades.

Sintra in the 16th century, like the town of Asolo on *Venetian terra-ferma*, was pre-eminently a place for country holidays and summer sojourns, and became a centre of *otio fecundo*[29] — high-minded cultural exchange, as defined by Pietro Bembo, the author of *Gli Asolani* (1505). Rafael Moreira, in a recent article, considers Sintra to be a perfect setting and back-cloth for a way of life as described by Baldassare Castiglione in «Il Cortegiano». The perfect courtier was

gracious and spontaneous in manner, as clever in letters as in war, versed in all the arts, from conversation to music and painting, and the ideal court of which he would be one of the stars, should be enlightened by a just and cultured prince, and be situated in a beautiful palace surrounded by hills, in some valley with a pleasant clime, watered by fountains, peopled by woods and flowers.[30]

The works carried out at the Royal Palace of Sintra in the first two decades of the 16th century show the beginnings of a domestic refinement and cultural sophistication during the period of King Manuel (1495-1521), and constitute the start of an interest in Sintra which developed through the reign of his successor, King John III.

Fountain with baldachin in the interior courtyard of the Torre de Ribafria, Cabriz.

Fireplace presented by Pope Leo X, found today at the Royal Palace.

The Heraldic Hall, Royal Palace of Sintra.

Buildings began to face outwards, breaking the massive solidity of the walls with wide apertures and porches. From now on the natural world outside gained particular importance and, at the same time, Sintra reached its peak as the centre for Renaissance culture. Witness to this are «the greatest number of Renaissance 'villas' in the country»[31] and the lengthy visits of numerous artists and well-known proponents of the classicist ideals.

The Manueline Court was pre-eminently wealthy, the period of economic development and maritime expansion having showered its protagonists in wealth and glory. The king, with his kindly disposition and «given to hunting and good food»... «stimulated life at Court, creating a cultural environment around him seeking the company of men of letters and foreigners with whom he always conversed and debated»[32].

King Manuel showed a particular fondness for Sintra and accordingly remodelled the town Palace which, since the time of King Dinis (reigned 1279-1325) had belonged to the Queen's Household.

The royal works of the Palace of the town of Sintra, accentuated in the first decades of the 16th century on the initiative of the king himself, who spent

The Swan Room, Royal Palace.

large sums of money on it and employed foreign artists, gave the old *Alcazar* of the muslim *walis* a new and dynamic look which can be seen in the Manueline wing on the East front, or in the famous «Sala dos Brazoes» (Heraldic Hall), where work still continued into 1517. [33]

Manueline architecture in the Palace of Sintra shows a new harmony: the geometry of its openings is leashed into strict patterns; decorated with plant shapes and nautical ropes or cables it simultaneously embraces the natural world, and pays tribute to the source of its creators wealth; it breaks through the mediaeval apertures creating rooms into which light pours, bringing with it the lavishness of the mountains as though an extension of the flower-filled courtyards. The whole Palace opens into the immensity of the hills, allowing itself to be taken over by the abundant tranquil and peaceful world outside, *datur orae serenas* [34].

Many of the parts of the palace which had been added or modified on the orders of King Manuel were given «Italianate» motifs and solutions in their completion or later decoration by his grandson, King John III who continued to develop the palace, building new rooms in a Renaissance style.

Torre de Ribafria in Lourel. Following page, *retable by Nicolas Chanterene in the former Pena Convent.*

In August of 1518, the Court moved to Sintra owing to the plague in Lisbon. King Manuel died in 1521 and King John III (the Italianophile) maintained his Court there. The delights of this region, described at the head of the chapter, appealed to the noblemen who were thus obliged to reside in Sintra and they began to found their quintas — the *Villa Rustica* of Renaissance Culture — in the outskirts of the town and from there to Colares. The dates of foundation of the various quintas reflect the growing importance of Sintra. These works were heavily influenced by the style of the Royal Palace, the King's master-craftsmen, or their pupils, supplying *«de buxos»* (sketches) to the courtiers, or even as we shall see in the case of Pêro Paixão working directly for the noblemen. Other artists who went to Sintra, with commissions from religious orders, would also influence the activities of the region by their presence. The schools and groups of followers formed by them brought about the expansion throughout that century of the new language of the Renaissance, although, in the *Villa Rustica*, in less erudite and less pure moulds.

The retable of the Convent of the Order of São Jerónimo da Pena, executed by Nicolas de Chanterene and finished in the reign of King John III (who placed an engraved inscription on it) was made between 1520 and 1532. The presence of this French artist must surely have contributed greatly to the Renaissance artistic culture in Sintra.

To a great extent we owe the introduction of the Renaissance love for the new artistic culture to Chanterene... and Master Nicolau assimilated the feel for the decoration and the forms of the Italian Renaissance to such and extent that we could almost swear that he had been in Italy, so perfect is his conversion to the new aesthetics, without even the slightest hint of gothicism[35].

An outstanding monument that represents the purest form of Italian Renaissance style, can be found on the landing platform by the fountain in front of the palace: a sculpted doorway of finest with marble, with «putti» and large spiral decorations rather like stylized vines. This is, in itself, such an obvious and accessible model that one wonders why there is none other like it or why it has never been copied elsewhere. It might not, of course, have originated in Sintra, as with the great Italian chimney-piece with caryatids, removed from the Palace of Almeirim[36] in the eighteenth century: tradition has it that this was a gift from Pope Leo X to King Manuel in 1515.

So let us leave these royal works for the moment to observe the example given by the noble families of Sintra and the courtiers. As Veríssimo Serrão says:

«it can be seen that the wealth of Lisbon came from its extremely rich surroundings, with many prosperous villages and six hundred quintas and country houses»[37] a great number of which were situated in the Sintra and Colares area.

In this context it is not surprising that one can find local families in the possession of considerable wealth and resources, such as the Ribafrias, owners of an important *morgadio*[38], later given the name of *Morgadio da Torre de Ribafria*. They also owned a great deal of land from Cascais to Ericeira and were the owners of an important town house close to the Royal Palace.

Courtyard of the Torre de Ribafria, Lourel.
Following page, *fountain with baldachin at the Casa de Ribafria in the Old Town of Sintra.*

To talk of the Ribafria family of Sintra is to point out a pattern of social advancement; they were rich landowners who held certain minor positions until, in 1518, Gaspar Gonçalves became Royal Chamberlain, and in 1541 the family was ennobled as Lords of Ribafria, by King John III. What was interesting in this evolution was that it was accompanied by a social statement which was simultaneously rooted in the old «seigneurial order» and in the modern way of life. Proof of this is to be found in the «old fashioned» tower of Lourel and the «avant-garde» house close to the palace. The former does not have the strategically high position which characterized true medieval towers, nevertheless it seems to imply an ancient seigneurial background. The latter example is obviously a compromise between its early origins and later development in that Renaissance part, «loggias», platforms and large openings to the exterior (in short, the «modern» spaces) command a greater presence.

The Tower attempts to show a strong relationship between the «solum», the *morgadio* and the owner's possessions. «These lands were called «solares» [39] deriving from the Latin word *solum*, which means land and seat, a man's establishment. They built where they lived, to defend themselves from attacks by the Moors, as was the way to build strong houses in the countryside, typical of the Northern nations, and as can be seen today all over France, Germany and England. In this kingdom permission to build these towers and put battlements on them was only given to illustrious persons such as those registered in the books of the nobility of the ancient kings. There are many of these «solares» and towers in Portugal, such as those belonging to the Abreu, Ataíde, Bayão, Britto, Carvalho families..., and many others from which these surnames derive.» [40] Thus, the Tower is an extremely important part of the social evolution of the family:

the manorial towers were therefore the noblest and most obvious sign of lordship over any land. [41]

The Ribafria morgadio, with its tower ruling over the estate and acting as it family *solum*, represented the ancient seigneurial tradition in the region. Once this stage of his social evolution was over and as a result of the King's evergrowing favouritism towards Gaspar Gonçalves, his assets rapidly grew and he was to become the fashionable owner of a *villa urbana* and a *villa rustica*. Certainly Gaspar Gonçalves' tendency to Renaissance ideas (which were also dear to the monarch and necessary to the courtly life which his post obliged him to lead) caused him, at a particularly high point of the new artistic life in Sintra, to remodel both his properties in an Italianate manner.

Breaking away from the massive tradition of Medieval construction, the Renaissance town-house is built around a patio, allowing all the sunlight in. The works were contemporary with the presence of Nicolas de Chanterene in Sintra and it is possible that he might have participated in their edification, not only because of their importance but also because of their novelty in style. The medallions in the inner «loggia», formed by three columns of marble with Corinthian capitals, seem to be attributable to him. The presence of another royal artist/craftsman is more certain. One of the capitals at the entrance to the mansion bears the following inscription:

This work was done by Pêro Paixão in the year one thousand five hundred and XXXIIII.

As a modern attitude of the affirmation of the artist (to which one might add veiled pride of the owner in possessing a work by someone who had worked in the Royal Palace) this capital is a revealing example.

From the location of the house on the hillside (which in itself shows a certain Italian influence, making full use of views), and the «open» style provided by the numerous *loggias* and windows, we can

say that besides the architectural design of the house there is a strong concern for landscape design.

The enclosed house gives way to a new concept by opening outwards, seeking a greater contact with Nature, piercing and increasing the openings in order to gain access to an interesting landscape. This new attitude is characteristic of the Renaissance. Nature, therefore, plays and increasingly important role in the concept of the house, and it is not surprising that the art of gardening developed from that time. [42]

This attitude was later extended to the Tower at Lourel, transforming its hostile and military exterior into a pleasant residence open to the landscape, converting the tower and all its surroundings into a *Villa Rustica*. In fact, the compromise of a vertical tower over a horizontal body already shows a late medieval, almost pacific character when considered as a whole. The care taken in the modular symmetry of the window-openings, which have but one central column, lends harmony and balance. The entrance to the palace is less affirmative of seigneurial character and gives a feeling of domestic docility, its ornamentation is at eye level and therefore is of human scale and greater interest.

Several authors have established comparisons between the urban residence in Sintra and the country seat of Lourel; in fact, the stylistic details of the tower are very similar to the work of Pêro Paixão at the town-house:

At the Ribafria house we find a beautiful Renaissance fountain with small columns supporting a canopy, situated on the terrace next to the inner patio. This fountain, which is purely classicist in the ordered simplicity of its lines, should be compared with another of identical characteristics, to be found at the Tower bearing the date 1542. [43]

It is possible that this dated fountain could also refer to the termination of the works altering the rough medieval tower into a suburban residence. That this is likely can be demonstrated from a study of the details of the tower. As we know from the quotation cited above from Severim de Faria, the battlements of this tower can only have been added following the ennobling of the family in September 1541. These crenellations incorporate a renaissance cornice which is in the style of the 1542 fountain thereby suggesting that all these embel-

lishments were made at the same time. Gaspar Gonçalves, rich landowner, was manifesting through these works his new status as Gaspar Gonçalves, Senhor de Ribafria.

So we learn that:

On 10th September 1541, Gaspar Gonçalves ordered the estate to be increased, at the same time (as the sovereign had done him the honour and favour of elevating him to a state of nobility with a coat of arms and a solar) taking the name of his estate as his surname and establishing the name of Ribafria for his descendants. The respective coat of arms bears the date of 16th September 1541 and is made by António da Holanda. [44]

It was also established that the *solar* and *morgadio* of the Ribafria family should be the said tower and quinta close to Sintra. [45]

As regards the outdoor spaces of the tower, particularly the garden, it should be remember that this was an agricultural residence: the entrance patio, nevertheless, seems to separate the refined interior from the coarse exterior.

No evidence remains to allow us to conclude as to the existence of gardens in this «rustic villa», other than by the nature of its appearance. As the residence of the *morgadio* one would suppose that it was surrounded by vegetable gardens, orchards and cultivated fields which by their luxuriousness must have been a place of pleasant Renaissance discourse.

Was there an attempt to evoke the patios of the Royal Palace? The fact is that the Royal Court had adopted new cultural values after Horace and Virgil, appreciating rustic life in its genuine simplicity and transforming orchards and vegetable gardens into extensive pleasure grounds. The natural world thus enhanced and complimented by Renaissance culture, constituted a total harmony with man.

> Populus Alcidae gratissima,vitis Iaccho,
> Formosae myrtus Veneri, sua laurea Phoebo.
> Phyllis amat corylos: illas dum Phyllis amabit,
> Nec myrtus vincet corylos, nec laurea Phoebi,
> Fraxinus in silvis pulcherrima, pinus in hortis,
> Populus in fluriis, abies in montibus altis:
> Saepius at si me, Lycida formose, revisas;
> Fraxinus in sylvis cedat tibi, pinus in hortis. [46]

The rustic houses (the «Quintas») scattered throughout Sintra and Colares were the residences of land-owning families in the region and

Torre de Ribafria seen from its garden.

Facing page, *main gate of the Quinta do Cosme, Galamares.*
Above, *entrance court of the Quinta do Vinagre, Colares.*

until this time had no architectural distinction. The frequent presence of the Court in Sintra, increasing the number of people residing in that area and diminishing isolation, contributed to the fact that these building began to develop signs of residential refinement.

The existence of schools of builders and stone masons who had been trained in the Manueline style and the new Renaissance art by the foreign-artisans of the erudite buildings gave the opportunity to the owners of these Quintas to make improvements to their own properties. In their general outline the buildings bear the marks of refinement with a humble simplicity, lending a soft air of nobility to the family residence.

Three adjacent Quintas on the old road from Sintra to Colares are homes of the landed gentry in the region, both as regards their chapels and their architectural detail: Quinta de São Bento, Quinta de São Tiago and Quinta da Infanta.

Gaspar de Cisneiros, nobleman of the House of the Dukes of Braganza, ordered the building of a chapel (now the Quinta de São Bento) in 1548. It was close to his house, the «noble and sumptuous» Quinta de Matalva. The style of this chapel was Renaissance with delicate medallions which clearly show the influence of the Sintra school of Chanterene. Prior to these works, however, there is here another notable building, of which only one room remains, it has decorated vaults and columns[47] in the Manueline style. The site is remarkable and the views of the «serra» and valley of Colares are quite splendid.

The neighbouring Quinta de São Tiago, although it has been considerably restored in this century, has managed to retain the atmosphere and details of an old Renaissance residence. The South — facing portico and the delicate stone balcony with hints of the Orient about it, the Chapel, and a monolithic rostral column are examples of the architectural interest with which simple farming residences became enriched. The Quinta da Infanta is across the road.

Further down the valley, with its gateways facing East towards Sintra and close to the river, are the ruins of the Quinta do Cosme. This property belonged to the Italian family of Cosme de Lafeta. The eldest son of that family, João Francisco de Lafeta had come to Portugal during the reign of King Manuel (1495-1521). He made his fortune by trading with India and subsequently left his business to future generations.

From the vestiges of the quinta which remain (a ribbed vault, a ruined tower and twin turrets appear to date from this period) it seems to have been a farm in which the owner's house was situated at the end of the main entrance-way with a large patio, typical of rural life, in front of the house. Also of interest is a well-proportioned, rather sombre seventeenth century gateway with the arms of the Lafeta family, who were ennobled by King John III (1521-1557).

In the direction of Colares, below the Quinta do Cosme, situated on a bend in the river, is the house of the so-called Quinta do Vinagre, *solum* of Dom Fernando Coutinho, Bishop of Lamego and Silves (died 1538).

Centre, *sixteenth century bridge adjacent to the Quinta do Cosme in Galamares.* Right, *architectural detail with the Lafeta family crest.*

Following page, above, *the arch of Quinta da Penha Verde with the cross unfortunately removed in 1988,* below, *view of the Quinta da Penha Verde* below left, *the Quinta do Vinagre in its oldest known photograph.*

The rustic patio with its noble line has a gallery with square pillars which dates back to the original construction; there are two lions facing each other on the central water tank, both holding escutcheons.

Another sixteenth century relic with and undertone of life as it was under the Spanish Philips[48] (when many noblemen retreated to their country properties), as is shown in an engraved tablet of Renaissance design attributed to Dom Fernando da Silva, morgadio of Vinagre:

«FORTISAM HIC LEVIVS VITE ERIT EXILIUM AMICIS ETIAM CLAVSA PATET 1586.»

This could be translated as follows:

Perchance that exile will be lighter in this place where our closed doors will always be opened to friends.

To what exile does the stone refer? Perhaps exile from Court, which at this date had been Spanish for six years. They would receive friends for whom the doors, which had been closed, would always be opened? Should one interpret the text of this stone as a patriotic outburst?

In Milides and Colares there are also vestiges of grand sixteenth century constructions, integrated for the most part today within buildings which show an eighteenth century design.

The most enlightened of the *villae* of the whole «serra» is also the simplest. Dom João de Castro (1500-1548), IV Viceroy of India, a nobleman of Renaissance education in its orthodox version of «virtu», may be considered a model of the true Classical man. His

Entrance to the Cork Convent, Serra de Sintra.

life is the very culmination of the classicist canons of Plutarch's *viri ilustrorum*, taking part in fierce battles in which he distinguished himself by his various feats and was always declared the victor. In his peaceful moments, he was a dedicated scholar of the Latin classics and of science, on which he was an authority. He had been a pupil of Pedro Nunes[49] with whom he consolidated his knowledge of Mathematics and Astronomy.

When he went to India for the first time he wrote copious information about the route and places visited, rather in the style of Pliny. He was a devoted servant of the Lusitanian Cause and for many years was Viceroy of India, his only reward, sufficient enough for him, being a small plot of land in Sintra set among crags: the Monte das Alvíssaras[50], where nothing grew except woodland trees, whose only fruit was shade. He gained not the slightest pecuniary benefit from this gift of the King's.

Following in Horace's steps:

But there is loyalty in me, ingenuity a bountiful vein, and the rich seek me out though I am poor; no more than this do I ask of the Gods, nor greater gifts do I ask my worthy friend; with the sole inheritance of the Sabine field am I quite content.[51]

With devotion he also interprets Ode XV of Book Two, letting his merits and virtues enhance society rather than raise a cumbersome monument, which would be the fruit of pride and an arouser of envy. This enables us to understand the humility of his house at Quinta da Fonte d'El-Rey (now known as Penha Verde), consisting of a simple single-storey house with vaulted roofs, today incorporated in the existing groups of houses. In 1542, he built a small

Chapel which testified to his learning. Rich in classical references, the Temple is a tribute of his scholarship rendered in homage to Nossa Senhora do Monte.

IONNES CASTRESIS CV XX ANNOS IN
DVRISIMIS BELLIS IN VTRAQ MAVRI
TANIA PRO CHRISTI RELIGIONE CON
SVMPSISSET; ET IN ILLA CLARISSIMA TVNE
TIS EXPVGNATIONE INTERFVISSET
ATQ TANDEM SINVS ARABICI LITORA
ET OMNES INDIAE ORAS NO MODO
LVSTRASSET: SED LITERARV ETIA MO
NIMENTIS MANDAVISSET: CHRISTI NVM
INE SALVVS DOMV REDIENS VIRGINI MA
TRI FANV EXVOTO DEDICAVIT
1542[52]

These are two other inscriptions:

SALVO, IRE   SOLVTIS.
SVSCEPTIS.   VOTIS
VOTIS. SAL   SALVOS.
VOS, IRE.   REDIRE.
1543[52]   REDIRE SALVOS.[52]

These inscriptions reflect the devotion of Dom João de Castro, but his gestures also show perfect harmony with the mythological suggestions of the metamorphoses of Ovid, a close follower of Horace and a cultivator of Virgil's lyrics.

Thus, as can still be appreciated today, trees were planted to gather shade, «The woods please us more than anything», and «Fountains full of moss, grass softer than the softest slumber, and the arbutus covers us with its fresh, sparse shade.»[53]

The Cork Convent.

When Beckford visited Penha Verde at the end of the eighteenth century he was to remember it as a landscape in the style of Gaspar Poussin, that is, as a perfect Arcadian setting.

Penha Verde itself is a lovely spot. The villa with its low, flat roofs, and a loggia projecting at one end, exactly resembles the edifice in Gaspar Poussin's landscapes. Before one of the fronts is a square parterre with a fountain in the middle, and niches in the walls with antique busts. Above these walls a variety of shrubs rise to a great elevation, and compose a mass of the richest foliage. The pines, which by their bright green colour, have given the epithet of verdant to this rocky point (Penha Verde), are as picturesque as those I used to admire so warmly in the Negroni garden at Rome, and full as ancient, perhaps more so. [54]

The «architecture» of the Viceroy's «villa» should be understood in its entirety, comprising: the hillside, the rolling, bucolic horizons stretching as far as the eye can see, the streams running between crags, and the rustic simplicity of the house itself. All «learning» was kept for the Chapel, as if learning only made sense in order to reveal Creation and generate harmony within the Whole. The round shape of the Temple allows for a deeper analysis and seems to say:

It is obvious that Nature is particularly fond of round figures, for if we see the greater part of things created, made or directed by Nature, we will see that they are round. I surely have no need to point out the stars, trees, animals, birds' nests, or other parts of Creation, to whom Nature gave a generally rounded form? [55]

Generally speaking the circular figure, having neither beginning nor end is a symbol of Eternity; it also underlines the one and only nature of Divinity in possessing one single geometric form. The design of the building is atributable to Miguel de Arruda, although a definitive study has yet to be made.

Inside the chapel against the wall are six delicate columns of careful workmanship. A finely sculpted cherubim completes the centre of the dome. Over the altar is a Holy Family — an excellent Italian sculpture of the period.

Here, beneath the shade of the trees, Dom João de Castro and Infante Dom Luís [56] must surely have enjoyed their *otio fecundo*, discoursing on the most varied and learned matters.

Álvaro de Castro continued his father's work, especially with the foundation (1560) of the *Conventinho dos Capuchos* (the Cork Convent), which perpetuated the «spirit» of Penha Verde on the other side of the Serra. Later, the Bishop Dom Francisco de Castro, grandson of the Viceroy, influenced no doubt by the charms of this spot, had three chapels built, but with comparatively less architectural interest.

On the Monte das Alvíssaras, a chapel dedicated to Saint Catherine was erected in 1638, as shown by the inscription. Particularly interesting is another chapel of this period which deserves a mention; here the decoration is made by encrusting the walls with stone, shells and fragments of glass. It is dedicated to Saint Peter, and has marble sculpture of the saint. He also built several fountains decorated with multi-coloured *azulejos* [57]. One of them has a panel with an abundance of animals.

The simplicity of the great Dom João de Castro's *villa* underlines the nobility of this period of Renaissance building. Much of this spirit would be carried forward through the next centuries.

ITALIAN, FRENCH AND ENGLISH INFLUENCES IN THE SEVENTEENTH AND EIGHTEENTH CENTURIES

B Y THE end of the sixteenth century the architectural «language», closely influenced by treatises of the Italian school which dealt with military architecture, defined a national style which was to be maintained during the seventeenth century until the first stirrings of the Baroque.

Philip I founded a new school of architecture, where artists were educated in the classical mould: an intellectual base founded as much on theory as on practical techniques. Works begun under this royal stimulus are to be found mainly in Lisbon, largely commissioned by the Clergy and Religious Orders. The era of the Spanish domination (1581-1640) is considered that of the «village court», as (with few exceptions) there was no spirit to build palaces and most of the nobility had decided to return to its country estates.

The many residences that had been built in Sintra during the reign of King Manuel (1521), King John III (1521-1557) and under the regency of Queen Catherine (1557-1562), when the court spent its summers there established not only a new style but also a new landscape within the rustic tradition of the area. In a document dated 1626, the Spanish architect Gomez de Mora, who came on an expedition to Portugal to describe the King's Palaces, said the following about Sintra:

Cintra has a large number of houses and gardens, where the Kings spent the summer, as it is very cool. It stands at the foot of a 'sierra' surrounded by peaceful quintas; it is the last promontory of Europe where Spain ends. [58]

The expression «peaceful quintas» is important: it shows the existence of a number of buildings which had begun to occupy the serra in the previous century, humanizing the hilly landscape and giving the scenery, improved by the introduction of gardens and orchards, an Arcadian air.

The quintas with their surrounding cultivation which gave them a certain «cared-for» look, lying between the woods of the 'serra' and the orchards of the valleys, characterized the Sintra landscape.

A widely-read Spanish book called «El Libro de los Secretos de Agricultura, Casa de Campo y Pastoril», published for the first time

Italianate busts on the gates of the Quinta Mazziotti, Colares.

in Barcelona in 1617, gives us a good idea of the gentleman-farmer brought up on Classics. He farmed in the wake of the Roman Emperors,...

and the ancient romans thought that rustic life should much be praised, more so than that of towns and villages. The greatest praise given to men was to call them good farmers, and he who was thus called was considered most honoured; and finally farming was held by the ancients in so much honour and esteem that the Roman Emperors themselves planted, sowed the fields, took care of the seedling and planted trees. They treated their hoeing implements with the same diligence and care with which they organized a field of soldiers.

Sintra, with its historic farming traditions, its special climate, sheltered valleys and reputation as a luxuriant place, was considered the ideal setting for this way of life.

During the first years of the seventeenth century, the town of Colares near Sintra benefited from the generous artistic and social protection of Bishop Dom Dinis de Melo e Castro, a remarkable scion of the Church, who acted as prince and patron of the arts. The Bishop gives us a clear example of life under the Spanish Philips, since he was born ten years before the loss of independence and died in the very year of the Restoration of the Portuguese Monarchy (1640).

All these influences prompted the Bishop to build a remarkable villa in the Italianate style in his home town of Colares. He acquired c. 1620, from the Town council, the ruined medieval castle of Colares on whose foundations he erected a sumptuous residence. It faced East, with uninterrupted vistas, open spaces for cultivation and leisure, and was elegantly planned, since then it has suffered greatly at the hands of both men and time; only the remains can be seen today (at the Quinta do Matias). These consist in a vaulted body with an outstanding terrace and a tall row of archways along the facade which bears the date 1690, no doubt the date of later alterations made by his heirs. Of the garden too, nothing remains except for some ruins. A great stone water-tank has frescoes and in-lays of extremely interesting mythological and pagan figures on one of its boundary walls, but they are in a state of decay. Secluded corners with patches of multi-coloured «azulejos» in «carpet» style and other signs of opulence may still be seen in this garden.

In 1623 the devout Bishop founded the Igreja da Misericórdia and the Hospital of Colares, attached to his property. In 1628, he appointed Matias Cristóvão as his agent for the Colares villa, who was to look after his affairs whilst the Bishop was in the Leiria Bishopric.

In 1638, the Bishop was also responsible for the vast stonework of the main body of the Parish Church of Colares (executed by the master stonemason André Duarte and designed by the royal architect

Portico surviving from the work of Bishop Dinis de Melo e Castro built over the ruins of the Castle of Colares.

Pillary (watercolour by
Fernando Perfeito de Magalhães)
and the Parish Church of Colares.
Below, a general view of the town of Colares.

Convent of Our Lady of Mount Carmel, Colares.

Pedro Nunes Tinoco). He also made additions to the Church of the Convent of Sant'Ana do Carmo, in Colares, where he is buried.

With the increasing stabilization of the kingdom following the 1640 Restoration, the Portuguese Court regained its privileges and there was a gradual revival of civil architecture.

During the sixteenth century the Palace of Sintra had been the centre of court life and on account of the works being carried out there, schools of artists: in the eighteenth century the centre of attraction moved first to Mafra and then to Queluz.

Under King John V, the works of the Convent of Mafra (begun in 1717) were the beginning of a new wave of Italian influence, later known as the Mafra School. The importance of the works brought

artists from all over the country, and developed the region around Mafra:

the small borough of Mafra became a city with forty thousand workers, a hospital, means of transport, etc. [59]

As pre-eminently agricultural regions, both Sintra and Colares supplied provisions for this extraordinary population.

Dom Jaime, 3rd Duke of Cadaval and John Frederick Ludwig, the architect of the works at the Convent, came frequently to the hills of Eugaria, near Sintra, doubtless in search of the coolness and peace they could not find in Mafra. Dom Jaime, director of the works at

Quinta da Capela, Eugaria.

Mafra, owned property in Sintra, hence the Duke was able to spend a great deal of time visiting his properties.

The works which characterize the architecture of the Quinta da Capela, belonging to the Duke of Cadaval, can be dated to the first and second decade of the eighteenth century. The style is rustic and sober in its outline, but its setting shows a sound architectural knowledge.

The place has an Italianate air, the cluster of stonepines which form an elegant «finale» at the bottom of the garden, behind the Capela de Piedade, are reminiscent of those in the Villa Medici in Rome.

The garden, the house and the outbuildings are built on the top of a hill on a wide terrace at the end of which is a large rectangular stone water-tank under the shade of cork-oak trees. Inside, a marbled

frieze on one of the dining room walls seems to recall the colour of the pink and orange marble of Mafra.

Further down from this Quinta in the direction of Colares and before coming to the small village of Eugaria, is the Quinta da Palma, which belonged to «Ludwig the Architect». Built at the same time (between 1715 and 1735) and consisting of twin rustic pavilions, it has a garden and terraces overlooking the valley of Colares.

The origin of this property lies in a gesture of kindness on the part of Dom Jaime towards Ludwig, as the lands belonged to his vast Cadaval estate in Sintra.

The site is excellent, the garden on the northern side unfolding in terrace slopes, with running water and fountains. Later, a baroque

Gardens of the Quinta da Capela.

Dining room, Quinta da Capela.

gateway, more fitted to the Queluz school, was to link the two pavilions and give them an air of grandeur which can be seen today. The Frenchified taste of Queluz which can be seen in the capricious undulation of the steps to the gateway, and the stone finishings no longer echo the serene classicism of Mafra:

Ludwig was not in favour of the curved and gracious forms of Bernini or Borromini. [60]

The type of construction in vogue in the «serra», illustrated by these two examples, was applied to the other Quintas. Building consisted mainly of rectangular structures, although some are «L» or «U» shaped, but always with sober stonework round the doors and windows. What distinguishes them from simple rural buildings is the size and regularity of the interior rooms, with coffered wooden ceilings, frescoes with bucolic scenes and some touch of architectural elegance, such as the plasterwork finishings of stone reservoir or of a gateway. The *Quinta do Vinagre*, which from 1713 formed the second *morgadio do Vinagre*

Quinta da Palma, Eugaria.

belonged at this time to Afonso Dyck and provides a good example of the development of a family house, agriculturally based and sited in the fertile valley. These buildings with their sixteenth century origins show this mixed language of semi-rustic and semi-erudite architecture. A further example of a farm embellished with sophisticated architecture is the *Quinta da Madre de Deus* with its superb chapel. The Quintas of *Rio de Milho* and *do Alto* allow us to complete the group.

1770-1790 saw the appearance of Sintra of new types of pavilions, houses which were greatly influenced in their decoration by the French. The *Cours d'Architecture* manual and the Vinhola Orders in the republished version of d'Aviler or the Jombert editions were made full use of. The local origin of the builders meant that many buildings were never possessed of strict or excessively learned rendition. A rustic air pervaded, making for a rather more homely character beneath that of the courtier.

The Quinta de São Pedro, belonging to the Marialva family, is a typical example of this:

A new creation, which has cost him a great many thousand pounds sterling. Five years ago it was a wild hill bestrewn with flints and rocky fragments. At present you find a gay pavilion designed by Pillement, and elegantly decorated; a parterre with statues and fountains, thick alleys of laurel, bay and laurustine, cascades, arbours, clipped box-hedges, and every ornament the Portuguese taste in gardening renders desirable.

This is no longer a rural building but a «pavilion», to be occupied occasionally during times of leisure. The size of the gardens further underline the importance of the exterior, so too the choice of the setting of the house, which is anything but agricultural, but all of beautiful scenery. Two other examples, both probably by the same architect, can be seen in the Quinta dos Freixos in Colares and the Quinta de São Sebastião in Sintra. Although both are different in size, they maintain the same idea of a pavilion and not a farm and both are surrounded by gardens with fountains.

In these latter examples we can see simultaneously two elements, opposed in theory, which are characteristic of the new styles. The doors and windows which show a tendency towards the *gothic* arch and the

View of the gardens of the Quinta do Vinagre, Colares.
Following page, *the riverside front of Quinta do Vinagre.*

Entrance gate of the Quinta da Madre de Deus, Várzea de Sintra.

neo-classical decoration of garlands mingle with the same simplicity that the botanic species grow in the garden. The Quinta de São Sebastião has a remarkable set of frescoes. The settings of the two are quite different, the Quinta dos Freixos nestles discreetly close to the Parish Church of Colares whilst the Quinta de São Sebastião rises proudly from its castle-like platform, resembling a lookout point, from which it may see and be seen.

It may be opportune to mention that the first example of this type of noble house which almost has the air of a rustic pavilion, built as early as the sixteenth century, was to be found in the Ribeira de Sintra and belonged to the family of the Counts of Redondo. Tradition has it that it began as a hunting lodge.

From the hunting lodge to rustic pavilion, to pavilions with French or English influences, and later the Arabian-style pavilions and chalets of central Europe, this model will continue until the end of the 19th century. These houses, not connected in any way with productive agriculture, but destined to provide elegant surroundings for recreation or moments of leisure for the aristocracy, payed homage to the «otio fecundo» and to all worthwhile pursuits. They were meant to

Below, *entrance court to the Quinta da Madre Deus.*
Following page, *view of the Chapel of Madre de Deus.*

provide the background for a freer existence, far from protocol and stimulated by the prodigal scenery of the «serra».

From mid-eighteenth century onwards, there was an increase in this attitude towards properties leading to even greater investments, more civilized gardens and more attention paid to the effect of the whole.

The works at Mafra and the school of French influence in Queluz came to influence artists who found Sintra to be a vast field of opportunity. One of the most significant examples of the growing importance given by these artists to the treatment of gardens is the Quinta do Mazziotti in Colares. Strictly speaking, we must bear in mind that this name was only given when this family of Napolitan origin married into the family who owned the Quinta, descended from a certain José Dias. Thus it was originally known as the Quinta do José Dias, and as such was named in the lithograph by Domingos Schiopeta.

Superbly situated, it enjoys multiple views of the sea, the hills and the «planalto». The gardens are Italianate in structure and made on terraces following the contours of the slope; they are traversed by a vertical axis which crosses the public way by an archway topped with a belvedere with a roof in the style of Mardel[61]. At the top of the hill is a picturesque octagonal gazebo. The novelty of these gardens, apart from their decorative style, lies exactly in that perpendicular axis made over the traditional use of the terraced slopes. The use of water, already much explored in the seventeenth century, constitutes less of a novelty. Major hydraulic operations were undertaken to collect the torrents from the «serra» and take them to a large stone tank and reservoir below the gazebo which contained a small fountain. The waters thus collected formed a great torrent of water under pressure which spurted in a three-tiered waterfall over a mythological figure and into a vast stone tank. The flow of water over the terraces of this garden recalls the grandiose landscape effects of the villas of Frascati or Tivoli.

This more vibrant and perhaps more active part of the garden is in contrast to another more contemplative area of chestnut woods and «sub tegumine» retreats, where stone benches covered in thick moss provide excellent viewpoints out towards the blue of the sea. A long level avenue between thick box hedges and umbrella pines, of which

Quinta de Rio de Milho, Milides.

only moss-covered stumps remain, links the house to the edge of the farm-land. At the edge of the property there were two busts on pillars, sadly now only one.

Once again William Beckford attests to the graciousness of the setting and reminds us that for the English traveller its decorative qualities had gone out of fashion in 1787; he preferred the more rural aspect of the property:

Quinta Mazziotti, Colares.

A favourite attendant (17) of the late king's who has a very large property in these environs, invited us with much civility and obsequiousness into his garden. I thought myself entering the orchard of Alcinous. The boughs literally bent under loads of fruit; the slightest shake strewed the ground with plums, oranges, and apricots.

This villa boasts a grand artificial cascade, with tritons and dolphins vomiting torrents of water; but I payed not half the attention its proprietor expected, and retiring under the shade of the fruit-trees, feasted on the golden apples and purple plums that were rolling about me in such profusion. The Marquis, who shares with most of the Portuguese a remarkable predilection for flowers, filled his carriage with carnations and jasmine. I never saw plants more conspicuous for their size and vigour than those which have the luck

Gardens of the Quinta Mazziotti in an engraving by Manuel Luiz.

Views of the gardens
of the Quinta Mazziotti,
Colares.

Following page, *Belvedere
at the Quinta Mazziotti
over the road to Penedo.*

of being sown in this fortunate soil. The exposition likewise is singularly happy; screened by sloping hills, and defended from the sea-airs by several miles of thickets and orchards. I felt unwilling to quit a spot so favoured by nature, and M(arialva) flatters himself I shall be tempted to purchase it. [62]

In October, Beckford returned to Colares on one of his excursions. The description he made of this landscape contains words of devotion to the prodigality of Nature:

The valley of Colares affords me a source of perpetual amusement. I have discovered a variety of paths which lead through Chestnut copses and orchards to irregular green spots, where self-sown bays and citron bushes hang wild over the rocky margin of a little river, and drop their fruit and blossoms into the stream. You may ride for miles along the bank of this delightful water, catching endless perspectives of flowery thickets, between the stems of poplar and walnut. The scenery is truly elysian, and exactly such as poets assign for the resort of happy spirits.

The mossy fragments of rock, grotesque pollards, and rustic bridges you meet with at every step, recall Savoy and Switzerland to the imagination; but the exotic cast of the vegetation, the vivid green of the citron, the golden fruitage of the orange, the bloossoming myrtle and the rich fragrance of the turf, embroidered with the brightest-coloured and most aromatic flowers allow me without a violent stretch of fancy to believe myself in the garden of the Hesperides, and to expect the dragon under every tree.» [63]

This region must have been the most natural of landscaped gardens, realizing one of the most fashionable styles, as disseminated by contemporary English and French writers of garden theory. The Elysian epithet illustrates exactly the natural bond between the orchard and the woodland which enchanted Beckford.

Quinta de Santo António, Eugaria.
Following page, *façade of the Quinta de St.º António.*

The earthquake which destroyed Lisbon on 1 November 1755 also greatly affected Sintra and Colares:

It was disastrous in Sintra, and attained degrees IX and X on the Mercalli scale in town, degree IX in Colares, Terrugem and Almargem, being less intensely felt in Belas (VII and VII).[64]

As a consequence of the earthquake many of the towns had their buildings destroyed, and reconstruction began soon after. The aftermath of the destruction was fatal for the preservation of the architectural quality of the buildings, as the purity of the lines was altered by the repairs which were intended only to start the buildings functioning again. The landscape suffered equally, since trees were required not only for reconstruction in the region, but also in Lisbon.

With relative speed, owing to the Marquis de Pombal's economic organization and to the reign of Queen Maria, the State and Nobility were able to leave behind the phase of the temporary shelter in Ajuda and re-launch the construction of dwellings and pavilions.

The end of the eighteenth century was a particularly generous time for Sintra for it saw the addition of two outstanding monuments, one of which has the most wonderful gardens, witness to the pre-romantic conceptions of the time.

Monserrate of Gerard DeVisme and Seteais of Daniel Gildemeester, are opposite examples both in architectural style and in the design of the gardens. Whilst one favours neo-gothic architecture and makes gentle use of the landscape, the other is more classicist and makes more vigorous use of the exterior spaces. Their complementarity illustrates concurrent fashions of the period and underlines the interest shown in Sintra by rich merchants from the capital. Knowledge and business exposed these merchants to new European trends, inclining each individual towards either this or that style, or, as in the case of DeVisme, to try out both neo-classic and neo-gothic styles.

Gerard DeVisme was an English Huguenot — a protestant refugee from a noble French family — who came to Lisbon in 1746. A millionaire as a result of the monopoly in brazilwood granted to his firm DeVisme, Purry & Mellish by the Marquis of Pombal, he built and developed his «seat», the Quinta de São Domingos at Benfica, four miles from Lisbon. This Quinta was acknowledged as one of the most splendid of its kind notable for its gardens which were described by William Hickey in 1782.

We had several very pleasant parties with Mr. DeVisme at a beautiful seat of his a few miles from Lisbon, where he entertained in a manner never surpassed and seldom equalled. The establishment was in every aspect princely, the house a perfect cabinet, the grounds laid out with peculiar taste, having in them the rarest plants of the European world and some even from Asia and America, but what delighted one was the songs of the nightingales innumerable pouring out their sweet notes in broad daylight. Mr. DeVisme told us that he had been at great expense in enticing them by curious strategies to his woods, but had at last so completely succeeded as to have their music full eight months in the year.[65]

What we would give to know the curious strategies necessary to attract nightingales!

In 1790, DeVisme was sixty-four and sick. His monopoly was becoming less secure after problems with the Queen, and it seems likely that, as Gildemeester in similar circumstances, he decided to retire to Sintra — both northerners, the climate and the landscape made it the obvious choice — away from the tribulations of Lisbon.

Dona Francisca Xavier Mariana de Faro Melo e Castro, the administrator of Monserate, was looking for a tenant to restore this isolated farm that had been destroyed by the earthquake of 1755.

DeVisme took a repairing lease in January 1790. This contract document has come down to us today (it was reprinted by F. Costa in his *Historia...*)[66] and is illuminating about the man and his motives for the move. He is described as «one of the most solid merchants» of Lisbon and characterised by his special genius for agriculture — an ideal tenant. He liked the remote situation that resembled his homeland and felt that it was likely to restore his health and provide relief from the fatigues of his business. He promises to enlarge the orchards and repair the buildings, and lastly to build a «decent house». The lease was to run for nine years with an option for a further nine — only 18 years, but a small concern for a man of DeVisme's age and means.

He set about his task rapidly, engravings of 1793 show the house and garden complete. His first act must have been rather alarming for his Catholic landlady, for he took down the chapel of Our Lady of Monserrate, founded by Gaspar Preto in 1540, to make way for his new house. In choosing this site he followed ancient tradition in garden-making: sacred spots of natural beauty were the first landscape gardens, the most famous example being Tivoli near Rome. Many such groves existed in Sintra: the Roman Temple of the Moon, Santa Eufémia, Peninha, and the Pena (itself to be developed into a great landscape garden). At the same time he followed a new fashion: the chapel was re-erected on a site in view of the house as a garden building. An object in the landscape.

DeVisme was an innovator in Portugal. José Augusto França has shown how the Quinta de São Domingos was the first Neo-Classical building in Lisbon and how the house that DeVisme built at Monserrate — a Mock-Castle — was the first Neo-Gothic structure. Both styles of Architecture were concurrently fashionable in England but DeVisme's choice in each case was in no way arbitrary. As an emergent figure wishing to demonstrate his status and culture in Lisbon the classical style is entirely appropriate. At Monserrate in the *Divini Gloria Ruris* (glory of the divine countryside) a less sophisticated more rustic style was adopted. In this way we see him acting as the Senhor de Ribafria, Gaspar Gonçalves, had done with his houses in the sixteenth century.

Quinta dos Freixos, Colares.

Quinta de São Sebastião, Sintra.

Frescos by J. B. Pillement at the Quinta de São Sebastião, Sintra.

His choice of garden styles to compliment these buildings follows the same argument. The rational exposition of botanical specimens in a formal layout was an extension of his classical palace/museum, «the perfect cabinet». In the wider countryside he applied his genius for agriculture to the expansion of the orchards and the raising of sheep (both are shown in the Noel print taken from the south published in 1795).

An agreeable retirement in the classical tradition of Virgil's *Georgics*, but the choice of the gothic style for the house and the re-erection of the chapel in the grounds give us an inference as to the garden philosophy of DeVisme at Monserrate.

As an Anglo-Frenchman he had a cultural background different to the garden-makers around him. The garden we see in the prints of 1793 and 1795 has details that suggest the existence of a «Ferme Ornée». This word was coined by Stephen Switzer in his *Ichnographia Rustica*. The term first occurred in the 1742 edition: «This Taste... has also for some time been the practice of the best Genius's of France, under the Title of La Ferme Ornée.» The idea had first been put forward by Addison in his famous *Spectator* essay in June 1712 «Why not a Whole Estate be thrown into a kind of garden by frequent plantations?... If the natural embroidery of the meadows were helped by some small additions of Art... a man might make a pretty Land-scape of his possessions.»

These «small additions of Art» at Monserrate were as well as the Castle and Chapel, a Gothic Tower, an Obelisk, a Roman Arch and a Neo-Classical Coach House (both these last still exist) all amongst the oranges and sheep of DeVisme's rural retreat.

There are important precedents to each of these features which were described in the garden literature of the time. Possibly the most influential of these theorists in the divulgation of the style in Europe was Thomas Whately. He wrote a rather old-fashioned manual of garden aesthetics and practice entitled *Observations on Modern Gardening* published in 1770 which went through several editions (the fifth was published in 1793). This book had a great influence in Europe through its French translation (1771) by Latapie, *L' Art de former les jardins modernes*. In it are described several gardens of a Gothic Inspiration including several Fermes Ornées: Hagley Hall a mid-eighteenth century creation with its «Castle» by Sanderson

Miller; the great landscape garden at Stowe with its Gothic Tower; and Painshill which had a Gothic Pavilion. The two Fermes Ornées: The Leasowes and Woburn Farm were described in some detail.

Was it possible that DeVisme had read this book? Thomas Whately wrote to Latapie that the book was unlikely to be under-stood by Europeans that had not been to England — whether he read the book or not DeVisme would have understood it: the garden proves it!

Whately's book was, as has been observed, «rather old--fashioned». And DeVisme though an innovator in Portugal was in comparison to his successor at Monserrate rather provincial. William Beckford had visited the Quinta de São Domingos and was rather disparaging about its «propensity to broken china».[67]

Beckford was his own genius; widely travelled and cultured and with vast wealth, he set about creating gardens in his own style. He has frequently been identified as a pre-Romantic and as such the attraction of Monserrate was its isolation and its natural beauty.

Beckford had seen, and coveted, Monserrate during his first visit to Portugal (March-November 1787), he wrote to Cyrus Redding (his biographer) that

It was a beautiful Claude-like place, surrounded by the most enchanting country. It belonged to a Mr. DeVisme, a merchant, of whom at the time I could not obtain it. Afterwards, however, he pulled down the house, and built another in barbarous Gothic. On my return I rented the place off him; for although he had pulled down the old edifice, he could not level the hills nor root up the woods. I built it! 'twas built by a carpenter from Falmouth.

Rather unfair comments since we know that the «old edifice» was in ruins, but Beckford was at pains to distance himself from what was indeed barbarous — in comparison to the gothic Fonthill Abbey that Beckford was to build in England (begun in 1793 and completed in 1813).

If we know little of DeVisme's activity at Monserrate then Beck-ford's work there is positively obscure: for a long time it was doubted that he really lived there. This is now proved by the existence of contract documents and letters written from Monserrate. In August 1795 he wrote to Sir William Hamilton of «my proceedings here in building and gardening etc.» and again in September of «having built

*Engravings by Baker
published by Wells,
showing Monserrate
and Sintra.*

Ruinous condition of the 'Castle' at Monserrate in 1859.

houses». The problem for the garden historian is to distinguish his work from DeVisme's.

The two prints of 1795, referred to above, are entitled *Mr. DeVisme's Residence* and must therefore have been drawn before July 1798 when the property was sub-let. Beckford retained the lease until 1808 but can only have resided at Monserrate between July 1794 and June 1796 and possibly during his third visit to Portugal from October 1798 to July 1799 — even during these periods he was travelling or living in Lisbon at times. A short period then, but no shorter than the time in which DeVisme had built the original house and garden.

By July 1795 Beckford was sufficiently pleased with his progress to invite his friends to stay, he wrote to Senhora Bezerra:

Monserrate with all its blooms and fragrance is at your absolute command whenever you choose to honour it with your presence... I have been too engaged with the Royalty of Nature, with climbing roses and cork trees, with tracing rills and runnels to their source, and examining every recess of these lovely environs, to think of inferior Royalties. Not once have I left this enchanted circle. Here I remain spellbound, and no talisman in the prince's power could draw me away... I have been extremely lucky in my choice of location which is as dry, as healthy, and as gloriously cheerful, as the most classical spots in Arcadia.

All this indicates that Beckford was happy at Monserrate but brings us no closer to understanding his garden. Five prints of Monserrate from after DeVisme's tenure exist, they are: 1828 from a sketch by the Rev'd James Bulwer; 1828, A. C. Barreto; 1830 — two prints published in «Portugal — The Young Traveller's Guide; 1840, Celestine Brelaz. What is striking is the gradual decay of the property over this time (see F. Costa, *A lenta ruína da Casa Castelo* in his *História*[68]) but that is not our concern. These prints show a

garden that — ruin apart — is obviously more «natural» than the Ferme Ornée of DeVisme. The path layout is retained but the outlines of the fields is softened by the new planting of woods and the radial axes have disappeared. The strange facade of the mock castle is harmonised by tree planting near to the building, integrating it with the landscape. Celestine Brelaz shows an ornamental lake low in the valley with the castle high above the surrounding woods: such as we see in later prints and paintings of Fonthill. This has the mark of Beckford.

It is this mark, this style that must guide us when looking to other garden features that are not shown in these prints.

> This choicest spot doth end, I ween,
> In a deep-sheltered cool retreat,
> Shadowed all o'er by Laurels green,
>
> Here Vatek sat, and did he use,
> Oft in the sultry noon to muse
> In this fastidious bower y-wove
> Of circling rock, and leafy grove,
> His own creation: mortals now
> Spread oft their rural banquets here
> And pour libations free their vow
> To Bacchus, and to Ceres, cheer
> Grateful in summer's thirst! Oh! green
> Retreat, all laurel-canopied
> Sun-shielded, charmed circle wide,
> To mirth devote![69]

A bower? Perhaps this was Beckford's, an Arcadian substitute for the oriental pavilion of Ramalhão.

On the shady side of the valley... you see a waterfall over enormous rocks, which were deliberately placed there, showing in this way how much labour

Above, *a crenellated turret, last vestige of the 'Castle' built by DeVisme at Monserrate.*
Below, *stables attributed
to DeVisme's tenure at Monserrate.*

is required when human artifice tries to imitate Nature's simplicity, always majestic and beautiful in the works of her creation; this dam takes its water from the top of the mountain which flow in winter and early spring and produce a cascade that hurtles down a rockly bed which makes up the valley floor. [70]

This magnificent cascade, which exists today, and still astonishes visitors when they are told that it is man-made was surely the *magnus opus* of Beckford at Monserrate — the result perhaps of his enquiries to the source of those «rills and runnells». Planted as a pair either side of this cascade are Stone Pines — Claude-like — as though memories of Italian Travels. Associated with it is a rocky arch which was described in 1870 by Thomas Cargill, as «Vateck's Rocky Bouldered Arch» indicating that by that time at least the work had been attributed to Beckford. The attribution is not unreasonable since the arch, of massive construction, bears a striking resemblance to the grottoes constructed by Josiah Lane for Beckford at Fonthill (c. 1794). Even more striking in its resemblance to Josiah Lane's work is the pile of rocks that stand, today incongruously, above the coach house on the side of the hill. A sublime detail.

a rude erection in imitation of a Cromlech is still today, equally forgotten, to be found at Fonthill. [71]

The Cromlech is however not the only «pre-historic» monument that Beckford created at Monserrate — what is regrettable is that it is only one that survives. A stone circle! Mystery and antiquity were two of the marks of the Sublime Garden. The force of the natural landscape with its rugged crags, reinforced by the torrential cascade provide for an awful contrast to the beauty of the natural vegetation; but a cromlech, and a stone circle: these are intellectual devices of awe! Again it is Thomas Cargill who records the existence of this stone circle. His directions are precise, and it is tempting to follow them, but how to find a circle of stones in a mountain of stones after 200 years?

Stand at the South Portico of the palace and look towards the mountains above the Estrada Velha:

> See'st thou, my Oberon! high on Mata's steep
> Bedded in verdure, yon particular stone?
> «Philosopher's» we term it — all alone,
> Flat, glistening white — none else around to keep
> It company: — thereon a Poet oft,
> Lost in deep-brooding thought, did used to sit.
>
> Above the Poet's stone, a winding way
> Few paces thence removed doth pleasant veer,
> Leading the pilgrim to a circle grey
> Of ancient stones,.......
>
> Memorial this of Vateck's taste and love
> For Beauty wheresoever her devious steps may rove.

Belvedere over the entrance to the former Quinta da Alegria, Seteais. Left, the «Rocky Arch» of Vathek.

Principal façade of the Quinta da Alegria during the time of its first owner Daniel Gildemeester.

A Stone Circle, a Cromlech, a Rocky Arch and Cascade in 1794 — the year of publication of Price's *Essay on the Picturesque* and Knight's *The Landscape*, a didactic poem — these features are not the work of a provincial merchant a few years from death. Beckford was exercising for his greatest work: *Fonthill*.

Daniel Gildemeester was of Dutch nationality, and during the time of the Marquis of Pombal he made an immense fortune out of the diamond monopoly granted to him by the Marquis, and his business activities, which he combined with the post of Consul of the Netherlands in Lisbon. He lived in the Janelas Verdes Palace overlooking the Tagus, a building in which he made many improvements.

No reason is known why he gave up all his business in Lisbon to settle in Sintra. We are led to believe that from 1783 onwards he wished to spend his remaining years in sweet leisure. He died in 1793.

An anonymous 1851 manuscript tells us that:

in 1783 he bought the cherry fields and woods at the end of the campo do Alardo which apparently had formerly produced barley... He ordered the large rocky mound there to be demolished and built the palace that we see today. [72]

Gildemeester was to become one of the great lovers of the «romantic»...

who made the Portuguese appreciate the sweetness of the air, the water and the seductive beaty of the Cintra 'serra',... and did all in his power to make it and his property famous *for up till then* its inhabitants saw very little, particularly in the years in which our kings did not go there.

The building he erected, in an extremely beautiful place, a true lookout point, caused him to undertake great efforts as was witnessed by the same source:

...he ordered the large rocky mound there to be demolished and built a palace that *we see today*

and further on

...on the North side of the palace between this and the kitchens (demolished by future owners) he built a small dovecote. The Quinta he called *da Alegria;* to build it he had many rocks broken and brought in a great deal of earth, made a large garden, diverted a large quantity of water from the serra, sowed and planted many trees. In the woods he also placed grottoes and belvederes, a bathing-house, large stone water-tanks, and orchards of citrus fruit trees.

One might think that the building now occupied by the Seteais Hotel was the palace of the retired Dutch Consul. In fact, only one part existed when William Beckford attended the inauguration in 1787. The rest was added by the second owner, Dom Diogo Vito, Marquis of Marialva; these were additions of such pure neo-classical style that a mature unity was achieved for this building of such strength that further alterations would be unthinkable.

Then are several structural details which distinguish, without doubt, Gildemeester's house from this later addition. For instance the quoins or cornerstones, the discontinuous and broken friezes (particularly on the south corner of the building) and the unbalanced plat-band of unusual height of the facade that faces the parterre. The original plan of the building was thus a simple «U» shape facing the terraced lemon groves and gardens. The internal geometry of the house and symmetrical position of the main staircase prove this argument.

And so we have William Beckford, the cultured English traveller, on his way to the inaugural feast on 25 July 1787. The description he has left us of the entrance to the Quinta da Alegria is almost cinematographic, so well-described and realistic are the details and the atmosphere.

Lithograph by C. Brelaz showing the neo-classical façade facing the Campo de Seteais. In the background one of the chapels of Penha Verde.

Main Entrance Hall of Gildemeester's Quinta da Alegria at Seteais.

Moving off the first opportunity, we passed through dark and gloomy lanes

(as still exist today). He proceeds...

We were near being jerked into a ditch as we drove to the old consul's door. [73]

This text confirms the location of the main entrance, that is, after passing under the small contemporary belvedere of the gate lodge by which access to the interior of the property was made, one turns sharply right and along a road on a level with the garden at the entrance to the belvedere. This road rapidly rises in relation to the garden in front of the house. For this reason Beckford, who had placed the Marquis of Marialva on his right in the carriage, became increasingly aware of the precipitous ditch to the left which deepened as they approached the front door of the consul's home. The noble Portuguese doubtless did not understand what had happened as on his side he saw the continuous retaining wall of the Seteais field which prevented him from looking over.

«The space before this new building is in sad disorder», wrote Beckford regarding the making of the terraces and steps which were then underway. The «Sketches» go on to say:

«The house has little more than bare walls, and walls not spendidly lighted up.»

Beckford's «Sketches of Spain and Portugal» were published in 1834 but written up from his diary of 1787. This diary was published in 1954, edited by Boyd Alexander, and gives more details of the event. For example, we find the passage referring to the ill-lit apartments in amplified form:

In several apartments — you will hardly believe me — one woeful candle depended from the ceiling in a solitary lantern. I leave you to represent to yourself the effect of this stable-like decoration.

This passage although apparently of little interest, describes the ceiling of the room on the lower floor to the right of Beckford's way in (today the Hotel Bar) which, if lit, would only allow for the suspension of one single central lamp, exactly at the meeting place of the ribs of the crossed vault. From this dismal entry, the Journal goes on to describe a very different scene:

Gallery of the Quinta da Alegria, today Seteais Palace, where, at the opening festivities of 25 July 1787, was placed the famous «dessert frame».

Previous page, *present-day view of the southern corner of the Seteais Palace showing the junction of the two façades. The disproportionately high cornice of the Gildemeester façade results from alterations made during the construction of the façade facing the Campo de Seteais by the Marquês de Marialva.*

Gallery and staircase to the principal floor, Seteais Palace.

There was a bright illumination, a profusion of plate, striking breadth of table, every delicacy that could be procured, and a dessert frame fifty or sixty feet in length, gleaming with burnished figures and vases of silver flowers of the most exquisite workmanship.

In the Portuguese translation of the journal, made by Gaspar Simões, there is a misinterpretation of Beckford's eighteenth century English. The words «dessert frame fifty or sixty feet in length», meaning a kind of sideboard, were translated as «o pudim armado de cinquenta ou sessenta pés de comprimento» — a sort of giant pudding!

So Beckford saw a sumptuously loaded sideboard some fifteen or eighteen metres in length. In attempting to imagine where such a scene could take place it must be concluded that the only place in the whole house where it could be installed was in the gallery — the only space large enough. Thus, he entered from the lower darker storey and went up to the main floor which was brilliantly lit and festive.

William Beckford's extremely observant and detailed report (even to exact dimensions) shows us from the sequence of events the indoor and outdoor layout of the house which Gildemeester had built at the end of the «Campo do Alardo».

The definition of the style of this house raises some difficulties, given the lack of concrete information as to the author of the project. The period saw the appearance of neoclassical architects and we are tempted to believe that there were strong English influences of a style close to that of William Elsden[74]. There are similarities of the facades of the Dutch consul's house with some of Elsden's projects, but there is no documentary evidence to support this theory.

The straightforward charm, the views of the distant horizons and the architecture which was very much in vogue at the time, are strong enough reasons to have tempted Dom Diogo José Vítor de Meneses Coutinho, 5th Marquis de Marialva, already a lover of Sintra, to buy the house from the family of the deceased Daniel Gildemeester. He proceeded to undertake remarkable works of improvement in 1802 and 1803.

These works transformed the Palace into what we see today, strengthening the neo-classical outlines of Gildemeester's building. As luck would have it, we found, in 1985, amongst some manuscripts of the Lafões family offered for sale by a Lisbon antiquary, a bundle of contract documents for these works. This find confirmed and proved what we already concluded from a careful study[75].

Thus, on 13 February 1802 a contract job was signed for

the Campo de Seteais to match with that same Palace... to the Portico and windows corresponding to the said Palace, which is already completed, and similar cornice on both properties...

On 21 May 1802 Francisco Leal Garcia received

... four hundred and eighty thousand 'reis' in coins on account of the building of the Triumphal Arch in the Campo de Sentiaes [sic] on the outskirts of the town of Sintra.

On 6 July 1802, Joaquim Timótheo da Costa, master tinsmith received payment «... for an oval Medallion cast in solid lead, and well finished, the said medallion containing the portraits of Our Most Serene Princes, Our Lords (Prince regent Dom João and his wife Princess Dona Carlota Joaquina)». Other documents attest to the most varied details of the constructions works.

Is it possible that works were in the hands of a plethora of professionals as mentioned in the documents, with no one person responsible for the overall execution? We believe not, nor could it be possible in view of the resulting architecture which is so sophisticated in its use of the Classical Orders. The strict regard for the detail of the building, the finishings, the implicit order in the pilasters of the trium-

Present-day view of the gardens at Seteais.
On the following page, *view of the Pena Palace with the triumphal arch of Seteais in the foreground*

*Principal façade of the Marquês de Marialva's
Seteais palace.*
Above, *Triumphal Arch of Seteais.*
Below, *detail of the italianate busts
on the arch at Seteais.*

AUGUSTO IOANNI, FIDELISSIMO PRINCIPI
REGENTI, LUSITANAE GENTIS SPEI, AMORI,

Pediment of the Triumphal Arch of Seteais

Medallion in lead cast by Timótheo da Costa designed by F. Leal Garcia.

phal arch, and the extension of the cornices, which lend character and nobility to the edifice, all point to such a conclusion.

The elaborate culmination of the Triumphal Arch inspired by the drawings of *amortissements* of the «Cours d'Architecture de Blondel», is the work of the sculptor Francisco Leal Garcia. Its geometry conforms to an imaginary pediment drawn according to the laws of Vinhola, and supported on the corners of the two flanking buildings.

Thus, through these works, the principal facade of the palace was turned through ninety degrees to face the Seteais Field. The prominence given to this facade would have been unthinkable in Gildemeester's time since the field was then used as a military parade ground for the King's troop.

The classical geometric design, underlined by the strong lines of the cornices, gives a balance to the new principal facade. The design of this project is seen to be more sophisticated the more it is studied: The triumphal arch of the facade constructed to honour the visit of the «Most Serene Princes» was, in fact, an elegant architectural device to overcome the problem of linking the two parts of the enlarged palace over a public right-of-way. This solution had been proposed for such a problem by Palladio in his *Four Books of Architecture*.

Research leads us to attribute this project to the Architect Costa e Silva. There are many reasons for this, ranging from the architect's work at the Capela de Marvila belonging to the Marquis of Marialva, to his predilection for triumphal arches (Ajuda and Black Horse Square). The resemblance between the Seteais arch and the main entrance to the Ramalhão courtyard has been pointed out by several writers. Brief research into the Costa e Silva archives led to the discovery of a sketch for the Quinta do Ramalhao, showing a version of the oval staircase at the entrance. If, as this discovery proves, Costa e Silva was architect for the main entrance of Ramalhão, then the clear likeness between it and the arch of Seteais proves the authorship of the latter.

Neo-classical cornice, adorned by busts attributed to Francisco Leal Garcia, above the façade by the architect José da Costa e Silva.

Belvedere at Seteais built in imitation of the gate house of the former Quinta da Alegria.

Busts attributed to Francisco Leal Garcia.

The Pombal Palace in Queluz, which is by the same architect, as also proved by the documents in his archives, was built in collaboration with the sculptor of the Seteais Arch, Francisco Leal Garcia. This artist (of the Mafra School) was always responsible for the sculptures in the architectural works of Costa e Silva. The female figures in the Pombal Palace are identical to the ones of the fountain in the garden at Seteais. Taken with all this evidence, the garlands of the new facade of the Seteais Palace, so characteristic of Costa e Silva's work such as we see at São Carlos, Runa and Ramalhão, appear almost as his signature.

This explanation shows the development of the Seteais Palace. All that we see today which lies to the right of the arch was newly built by Marialva, the part to the left was the work of Gildemeester as modified by Marialva. Is it possible that a clue to this evolution was built into the main facade?

A pair of busts in the style of the Mafra School top the constructions on either side of the triumphal arch in Steais. Strangely, on the left side there is the figure of an old man with a beard and of a young girl. Marialva's addition bears the busts of two youths. Why are these busts not all old or all young and why this distribution? We believe that we have found the reason which, although merely speculative, is perhaps true: *all which is on one side has something old and something new — the other side is all new.*

Monserrate and Seteais, complementary expressions of the love for Nature held by their pre-romantic occupants, show the aesthetic sensibility of the end of the eighteenth century. The Romantic travellers, beginning with Byron, found in Sintra the «ideal landscape» that they had imagined. This put Sintra on the map of the European Romantic Pilgrimages, establishing its new identity.

ROMANTIC SINTRA

ROMANTICISM owes its principal devotion and stimulus to the landscape; it is not strange, therefore, that Sintra should have constituted a particularly ideal background for this period. Although off the beaten track of the Classical European Grand Tour from the geographical point of view, it was to figure prominently in the Romantic «tournée». Byron in 1809 immortalized Sintra in resonant stanzas. Beckford, in his «Sketches of Spain and Portugal» described in poetic prose his life in the Sintra of 1787. The preface to his work, not published until 1834, describes how much things changed in the interval:

Preface to Portuguese Letters: Portugal attracting much attention in a present convulsed and declining state, it might not perhaps be uninteresting to the public to cast back a glance by way of contrast to the happier times when she enjoyed under the mild and beneficient reign of Dona Maria the First, a great share of courtly and commercial prosperity.

The first decades of the nineteenth century were not peaceful ones for the Portuguese State. The French invasions from 1807 to 1810 threatened the stability of the kingdom, the Court left for Brazil and later the Liberal struggles plunged the country into a state of civil war. Whilst the Portuguese suffered the consequences of this instability, foreign travellers caught a glimpse of many curious aspects of a society under violent change.

Meanwhile, Sintra gathered much praise for its charm. Visitors, surprised by this «find», felt a certain perplexity, as if it were the rediscovery of a grandiose monument of which all traces had been lost. At the beginning of this century travelbooks and Romantic pilgrims spread the word about Sintra. Assiduously frequented by «elderly nobles, English travellers on Byronic pilgrimages, diplomats — the fame of Sintra grew. Then came the constitutional capitalists, following the rhythm of their expansion in Lisbon». They stayed mainly at the Lawrence Hotel (known as the oldest boarding-house in the country), and later at the Victor Hotel, at the Nunes and the Netto.

Apart from the families who already possessed properties in Sintra, in the 1830's an important Portuguese personality came to

Araucaria
at the Quinta da Piedade,
Eugaria.

Three of the principal hotels of Sintra.

Mrs. Oram with her guests at the door of the Lawrence Hotel.

Quinta do Saldanha, Old Town of Sintra.

live close to the Fonte da Sabuga, where he built the Quinta do Saldanha which housed all his art collections and family archives. General Saldanha had been coming to his estate since 1827, but it was only in 1834 that he had a mansion built in eclectic Romantic taste; it looked out towards the Palace in the town and the «planalto» to the North of the «serra». The neo-classic style shown by the construction at the gate entrance is in keeping with the inscription on the fountain, which is in the neo-Manueline style. The house itself was built in the neo-gothic style. All these are suggestions for a man who fell in love with the Romantic spirit of the «serra» and built an historical framework into his architecture. A significant gesture is that

represented by the removal of a Manueline gateway from the Penha Longa Convent, in 1836, and which he placed in his house.

General Saldanha had bought the Penha Longa Convent following the suppression of the Religious Orders in May 1834, when all religious buildings were put up for sale. The Convents of Trindade and Carmo also became residences.

Thus Dom Fernando Saxe-Coburg Gotha was able to acquire the small convent of Nossa Senhora de Pena. Founded by the Hieronymites and restored by King Manuel I in the 16th century, it was in a state of ruin following the 1755 earthquake, as can be seen in certain engravings.

The first engraving made of the Pena Convent, which shows it state upon acquisition by King Fernando II.

The Pena Palace during construction.

Dom Fernando, the Prince Consort, had renounced his family assets on marrying Queen Maria II, and was compensated by an annual allowance. From this income he bought and intended to restore the picturesque little convent. It was to serve as a summer residence; purely for pleasure.

This action of so distinguished a person served to draw people's attention once again to Sintra, as a place of Romantic charm and leisure. His gesture has been recognized as the stimulus of the new «occupation» of Sintra from 1840 onwards.

The gothic Pena monastery then shed its monastic simplicity to don the garbs of the century; it put aside the device of the sons of St. Jerome and decked itself with the coat of arms of Portugal and Coburg; it exchanged its dormitories and narrow cells for spacious halls; and in place of the humble name of monastery it took the pompous one of Royal Palace.

Then the august renovator of the Manueline monument made new and more splendorous additions to the old. At the same time as the old building was rejuvenated, as if by magic, a superb and wonderful palace arose, a true fairy mansion. And large tracts of the «serra» round the palace, acquired on several occasions by the royal founder, were transformed into a regal park, where the finest taste presided over its layout and landscaping. [76]

These ruins at the top of the «serra» were more to Dom Fernando's taste than placid Monserrate, which he had been tempted to acquire.

The Prince Consort was aided by Baron Eschwege in the construction of the palace, the first phase of which lasted from 1839 to 1849.

The career of Baron Eschwege was an adventurous Romantic pilgrimage from the Rhineland, where he was born, to Brazil and Portugal. Although not an architect himself, he had some experience in construction work and particularly in military engineering and mines. What is perhaps remarkable is that he was the vehicle of the first germanic concepts as regards the conservation of monuments.

The wave of restoration of gothic Rhine castles following the works of Friedrich Schinkel, the architect, had capture the Baron's attention. When he was given the opportunity of working with Dom Fernando, he drew up for him a fantastic dream of a medieval fortification, in a style similar to what he had seen, to be erected over the Convent.

Dom Fernando had wisely understood national architecture and had interceded in the conservation of several remarkable monuments of Portuguese genius (curiously enough most of them are now included in the World Heritage List). He stayed in the Royal Palace of Sintra during his visits to the works in Pena and this must certainly have influenced him to soften the gothic Germanic language of the Baron's project, replacing it with what was almost a repository of the

Building the Pena Palace, the construction of the great circular tower is in progress.

great Portuguese national styles. The Convent already had valuable works of art from the various periods of its history, such as the alabaster retable by Chanterene, and the elegant Manueline cloister. It was therefore not inappropriate that the project should continue in this vein.

The arab and *mudejar* (Hispanic Moor) style with domes and gateways and geometric decoration, the neo-gothic and the neo-Manueline, the neo-Renaissance of the South facade and the gate on the drawbridge which is reminiscent of fortifications covered in diamond shaped studs were all built in as though they had been phases in the life of the building. With reference to this Rackzynski made a caustic observation: «In 2245, archaeologists will puzzle over the dates of the different constructions.» [77]

After Eschwege's final departure for Germany in 1849, the works only started again in 1868 from which time they continued until the King's death in 1885.

Although the works were carried out at the same time as the restoration of Hohenshwangau, Pena Palace is some thirty years earlier than the castles of Ludwig II of Bavaria. The recovery and integration of the phases of Portuguese architecture and its values is in itself innovative.

Let us leave this profusion of detail which is soon lost between the mists and the horizon, with the silhouette of the palace, majesti-

cally and serenely crowning the «serra». In fact the mountain-tops seem to stretch upwards until they reach the ideal balance and complete fusion with the palace. The palace is not an imposition on the «serra», but rather its continuity. From whichever side of the mountain we look, it always presents a new version of its turrets and keep.

The greatest novelty is this integration in the landscape, one of the best examples of European Romantic architecture, Pena Palace, and the gardens and park surrounding it, constitute a grandiose work of *landscape* architecture.

Dom Fernando's botanical intervention in the «serra» was vast and the full tree-cover we see today is owed to the persistent and aesthetic efforts of the king. The Parque de Pena, occupying an area of 270 hectares, makes use of the valleys where the temperatures are never too low and where it is possible to grow rare botanical species, one of the king's favourite occupations.

As we have seen, the Castle of King Ferdinand II (Dom Fernando II), although with its profusion of Manueline and Moorish detail, was the fantasy of a northern mind. The integration of this «dream castle» within the southern landscape results from the remarkable opportunity presented by the climate of this mountain and the size of Dom Fernando's conception.

The Moorish Salon at the Pena Palace. Following page, *the dining room of King Fernando II, the old monks refectory.*

Dom Fernando had a remarkable site for his project, a combination of awesome grandeur and beneficient growing conditions which allowed him, as king, to develop a landscape equal to the scale of the Romantic imagination. What we see at Pena is not so much a garden as a whole landscape. The entire mountain, once «three shattered pinnacles of rock» was rapidly transformed. The castle rises above a forest of dark evergreens — seemingly transplanted from the Black Forest — but the pines and firs of Pena are exotic as the palace itself, this boreal scenery is composed of Mexican Cedars, Japanese Pines and Chinese Yews... and Portuguese cork trees.

The palace and garden were conceived as a whole: the influences that led to the fantastic form of one are to be found in the other. The park of Pena, as we have said is rather more landscape than garden, but within that landscape there were gardens: this is entirely characteristic of the «Englischer Garten» of the mid-nineteenth century. It has been suggested that the Castle-Manor at Potsdam reconstructed by the architect Karl F. Schinkel (1827-43) for the future Friedrich Wilhelm IV — visited by Baron Eschwege during 1830-34 — was one of the sources for the design of the Pena Palace. (Schinkel also designed the neo-gothic Schloss at Babelsberg 1833-34). The Castle-Manor was itself surrounded by a new landscape park, the Charlottenhof, designed by Peter Josef Lenne from 1826

Queen Amélia's writing desk with a portrait of her husband King Carlos I.

Private sitting room of the Royal Family.

Sundial on the Queen's Terrace at Pena Palace.

onwards. The most influential German landscapist of the time was Prince Herman of Puckler-Muskau. From his practical example on his estates at Muskau (1815-45) and Branitz (until his death in 1871) and from his book *Andeutugen uber Landschtsgartnerei* (1834) the Prince developed ideas obtained during his trips to England. The illustrations to this book may be compared to the garden details of the 1855 projects of Eugen Ruhl for Pena.[78] Puckler-Muskau wrote:

I always give a firm and definite form to individual flower beds, and prefer to enclose them in a framework of iron, wool, earthenware, or trellis.

The water-colours of Ruhl show these edgings and also interestingly Dom Fernando's monogram in flowers: Prince Herman had the letter «H».

The garden buildings shown in the Ruhl album, with their Moorish inspiration again returns to a southern style. Dom Fernando's fascination with the Arab world was exercised in the garden as much as the palace. The Fonte dos Passarinhos (fountain of the little birds) built in 1853 is unlike the tent-like structures of Ruhl and has more of the ponderous style of Eschwege, but is also built as a «Mosque», and bears an Arabic inscription:

The Chalet of the Condessa d'Edla
within the Pena Park,
shown in a late nineteenth century photograph.

A fantastic castle
crowning an exotic forest.

The Sultan Manuel I built this chapel dedicated to Our Lady of Pena, in the year 1503, in commemoration of the safe return of Vasco da Gama from his discoveries of the Cape of Good Hope and India. Then his Highness the Sultan Fernando II Consort of Her Majesty Queen Maria II ordered the reconstruction in royal magnificence in the year 1840.

Built in this manner of royal magnificence, the Pena is one of the few remaining great Romantic Landscapes in Europe.

The Quinta do Relogio and Monserrate characterized by their pavilion-like forms, were built in the 1850's and 60's. Both constructions bring to Sintra the Arab and Arab-Indian style, not as elements in an eclectic whole but as an architectural unit.

The new Quinta do Relogio took its name from an earlier building on the site which had a bell tower and a bell which rang the hours «to the sound of several minuets». It has an unusual design by the architect António Manuel da Fonseca, with inspiration from the published engravings of the time of Arab buildings. It has a higher central body with columns and on the ground floor the archways of the pavilion are horseshoe-shaped. The facade is decorated in horizontal stripes.

From the 1840's onwards, archaeological research and the advance in the study of monuments of various styles were published

The Chalet of the Condessa with the Palace behind.

Quinta do Relógio, Sintra.

in numerous works which became bibles for artists and models for many buildings. The dissemination reached its peak with the French, English and German folios, from the 1860's onwards; such publications as «Petites Maisons de Ville et de Campagne, gravées aux traits d'après les dessins originaux» or «Villa and Cottage Architecture; select examples of country and suburban residences». They display a range of fine engravings which were important models and sources of reference for patrons and artists alike.

Although the gardens of the Quinta do Relogio are not extensive, they are built round a picturesque lake, and have a modest collection of botanical species, possibly obtained from Monserrate and Pena. One should not overlook the ancient cork-oak tree to whose branches cling small Davallia ferns, which seem to find serene protec-

tion in this secular tree. Both Beckford and Southey mentioned the picturesque effect and old age of the tree.

From the point of view of aesthetics two gardens extend the possibility of Sintra. One, the Pena, towards the sublime, the other Monserrate, to the beautiful. The two gardens have more similarities than differences (as witnessed by the intense competition between King Fernando and Francis Cook over botanical rarities). The similarities come from the aspirations of the Romantic age, the opportunities of plant discoveries and the beneficient climate; the differences are cultural — the forests of Germany and the woods of England — and topographical: Pena is a mountain-top, Monserrate is a vale.

There is another essential similarity: *the best gardens are not made they are found;* both gardens are inconceivable without the

Ancient Cork tree at the Quinta do Relógio.
Following page, a view of the Serra at Monserrate.

natural profusion of beauty that suffuses and surrounds them. The both of them demonstrate the Romantic ideal of a garden dissolved in the Landscape; there are no boundaries, no limits: between the gardens and the garden landscape of Sintra to the very Atlantic.

Francis Cook and his Anglo-Portuguese wife Emily Lucas found Monserrate whilst honeymooning at the adjoining Quinta de São Bento. Still much as Byron had described it in 1809, they fell in love with it and this magnificent site was to enter upon yet another phase of development.

Like DeVisme and Beckford before him, Cook was an exceedingly wealthy man. Like them he rented the estate and set about restoring it. But circumstances had changed, the old law of entail had been abolished, and he succeeded where they had failed, buying

property in 1856. Francis Cook, later Visconde de Monserrate (1870) and Baronet (1896) set about establishing his Portuguese domain.

Eventually the Visconde was to found a dominion around Monserrate comprising thirteen quintas, a convent and a large slice of the mountain: Quinta de São Bento; da Infanta; da Cabeça; da Ponte Redondo; da Bela Vista; de São Tiago; de Pombal; das Bochechas; da Boiça; the large and small quintas Quinta Grande and Quinta Pequena; the Cork Convent; and the quintas do Conde e da Sanfanha. Within this demesne grew up a significant settlement dependent upon the estate: the village of Galamares. The Cook family was characterised by, and is remembered for, its generosity towards the people of Sintra: schools, houses and a theatre were built as works of benefaction.

An accurate picture of what Cook found at Monserrate is given by the engraving of 1859 in *Illustração Luso-Brazilleira*. The Castle stands, roofless, window-less, surrounded by the scrubby remnants of Beckford's garden. But time no more than DeVisme, could not «level the hills, nor root up the woods» the beautiful Claude-like place and its enchanting surroundings still remained.

Cook brought his architect James T. Knowles Senior, out to Sintra to survey the ruins (probably in 1857 or 58) and preliminary drawings were made in 1858: an elevation and a section showing the new form that the building was to take. Though the eighteenth century walls and window openings were to be retained the proposal was of an entirely new character. In place of the massive crenellated towers were airy domes giving a new lightness of aspect. The chosen style, eclectic, an extravaganza of Moorish and Indian, of columns and arches decorated with delicate traceries, Monserrate presents a mixture of imposed conditions and fantastic invention. The drawings having been made there was then a long period of delays, possibly for legal reasons. During this period the architect was working on the Grosvenor Hotel — considered his masterpiece — and many of the details of that building were to reappear at Monserrate. In her biography of the architect and his son J.T. Knowles Junior, Priscilla Metcalf considers the sources of inspiration for this extraordinary design. The illustrated periodicals of the time reflect a new interest in oriental art, particularly — in England — that of India. The books of James Fergusson describing oriental architecture were very influential. Such details as the window tracery and the eyelid windows shown in the elevation, the cupolas of the domes — Metcalf describes them as «Bandstand Orientalism» — and the fake-chimneys — «Victorian-Mughal microcosms that Loudon would have liked» — all add to the Indian character of the building. The most influential single building of an Indian style in England was the Brighton Pavilion. Stone lattice work occurs in the heads of the arches of both buildings, but the relationship here is one of idea rather than detail: the solidness of the eighteenth century walls prevented a closer comparison.

This solidness required a different technique. Knowles' response to the mock-castle's form seems to have been to emphasise the three towers as separate pavilions, each with their dome and cupola. Thus the central block is given a portico to emphasise its mass and the connecting galleries are treated almost as colonnade with their rows of arched windows. If this interpretation is correct then it was later reinforced by the way in which the gallery walls were made green with creepers whilst the circular towers and central pavilion were left clear. Read as three separate units Monserrate has a beauty that seems to have been unfairly dismissed by twentieth century critics.

Construction begun in 1863. As before, a contractor was sent out from England: J. Samuel Bennet (Later to work for King Fernando at Belém). The building took two years to complete and at its peak is said to have employed 2000 men (though no doubt many of these were employed on the garden). The craftsmanship and materials used in this reconstruction were of the finest quality: marble columns and traceries, intricate stuccos, a beautiful pinkish granite for the facing of the walls; it is easy to appreciate why so much work was required. The building was to be a gallery for a minor part of the great art collection of Francis Cook (his principal collection was at Doughty House in Richmond England). Classical sculpture lined the central gallery, tapestries and paintings were hung over the floral plasterwork of the main staircase and fabulously carved Indian furniture (each table seemingly a man's life-work) filled the rooms, the Indian motif was continued by the pierced screens brought from Delhi in the hall and around the balustrade of the main dome.

This decoration of the rooms, with its mixture of classical and oriental themes provides a clue to the effect that Cook intended to create but the stylised patterns of the stuccos and the stiff floral capitals were of an altogether English design, rather of an Oxford-School parlour room. The exotic ideal aspired to in the building was to be fully realised in the gardens around them.

The gardens of Monserrate were to become world-famous, mainly because of the fantastic variety of plants, from all over the

The original project drawings by James T. Knowles, sr. of the Monserrate Palace, for Francis Cook in 1858 (Courtesy of Brenda, Lady Cook).

South-facing door, Monserrate.

The central dome of the Monserrate Palace, seen from the road to Colares.

Indian gateway in the gardens of Monserrate.

Detail of the stucco work.

world, that thrived in its unique climate. Unlike the palace the gardens were made over a long period of time (1863-1929). The history of their development is a fascinating puzzle. Their design is generally attributed to William Colebrook Stockdale, a landscape painter in the Romantic style and it is certain that their picturesque quality results from his work. But Stockdale was, by his own words, in Portugal during 1873, 74, and 75 and thereafter; the early development of the garden was by another hand. It seems likely that during the first ten years — and in this climate ten years is a long time in garden--making — that Francis Cook was advised by his friend Thomas Cargill, M.D., a Lisbon doctor.

The earliest photographs of Monserrate were published, in 1870, as illustrations to a bizarre poem: *Fairylife in Fairyland* by Thomas of Erildonne[79]: three hundred pages of excruciatingly bad rhymes inspired from a single line of Byron

Thy Fairy-Dwelling is lone as Thou[80]

The fairy-dwelling was Beckford's and Fairyland is therefore Monserrate. The poem is an allegorical description of the opening festivities of Cook's new «palácio». In the poem Cook figures as «Orion» and his gardener, Francis Burt as «Vertumnus». «The good De Vim» and the bad «Vatek» are both given their parts as founders of the palace but there is no character that can be identified with the landscape designer Stockdale. The narrator, «Rhyming Thomas», has been identified by the late Ida Kingsbury as Dr. Cargill. A friend of

Cook, and probably of the Lucas family, Cargill would have been present at the inauguration and the attribution seems likely.

The poem is divided into three parts: the first describes the area of Sintra; the second the palace (dwelling with cabbalistic monotony of the numbers of arches); and the third, most interesting part, describes the gardens. Here we see that the basis of the garden is programmatic rather than picturesque, there are two overlapping programmes. The first is mythological and follows the progress of the Ancient Greek river «Peneus» from its source of Mount Helicon (This was Beckford's cascade). The second is a geographic designation which was to order the planting of the vast variety of plants. The garden was intended to have both a spiritual and a scientific structure: entirely Victorian.

Mount Helicon was a sacred mountian, at its foot rose the font of Hippocrene, made by the stamp of Pegasus (the corresponding pool at Monserrate is horseshoe-shaped), from which flowed the noble Peneus through the Vale of Tempe and past the Mount of Parnassus and the Font of Arethusa. All these features are represented at Monserrate. The classical sense of the garden is further reinforced by the presence of three Etruscan Sarcophagi, purchased by Cook from the Campanari family in the 1860's, that are placed in grottoes or bowers around the garden.

The geographical zones of the garden were carefully selected for their microclimatic conditions to meet the requirements of the flora of their respective countries. The poem described «golden» Australia and luxurient Mexico:

Views of Monserrate by William C. Stockdale (Courtesy of Brenda, Lady Cook).

Portrait of William Colebrook Stockdale,
one of the mentors of the garden of Monserrate
(Cook family photographic archive).

Lo! Mexico
Rock Strewn, in front of thee! what colours glow
On his hot surface! All that cactus gives,
Of indescriable painting, gorgeous lives
On his steep slope, and Aloe's flaming head
Shoots darting upwards from his rocky bed,
And Yucca's thousand chalices of snow,
Hang bending o'er those broken depths below
Outpouring all their sweets on fragrant Mexico!

A deep humid vale was chosen for the newly obtained treasure
from the Himalayas: Hooker's Sikkim Rhododendrons. These would
have merited special pride in this garden since they are too tender
to grow outside safely in England. Later additions to this geographical
system, not described in the poem and therefore difficult to identify
were Peru, Chile, Japan and others.

The mention of Hooker, a director of the Royal Botanic Gardens
at Kew in London gives us a clue to the source for the plants of this
early garden. It is known that William Nevill, a fellow of that institu-
tion also advised Cook — presumably on the botanical aspects of
his creation. Nevill rented the Quinta de São Tiago (added to the
Monserrate domain in the 1870's) from Cook; there are today many
plants in that garden, including an ancient cycad and many trees,
from his tenancy. An article in *The Times* by Sir J.C. Robinson,
keeper of Queen Victoria's paintings at Windsor, and adviser to the
Cook collection tells us that the Botanic Gardens of Lisbon and Rio
de Janeiro also contributed.

However Cook was quite venturesome in obtaining plants for his
new garden. He transplanted a giant Date Palm,

Probably a few hundred years old and the only one ever known in Portugal
to bear dates.

from Cascais to the garden in 1866. The plant was still thriving four
years later, a testament to the skill and care of the head gardener
Francis Burt. Perhaps this was the very palm that Beckford had espied
through his telescope in 1787[81]! But this was a small effort
compared to Cook's enterprise to obtain Tree Ferns — today perhaps
the most characteristic motif of the garden.

Faries! those self-same fern-trees that ye view
So old, so tall, in Dandenong they grew.

A note to Cargill's poem explains: «This was an experiment made two or three years ago at Monserrate (ie 1867-68), and it was then, I believe, new in the history of Fern-trees. Twelve fine Fern-trees *(Cyatheas* and *Dicksonias),* about eight feet (2.4m.) high, were cut down in the mountains of Dandenong, fifteen miles from Melbourne, and brought to London. They had been cut down level with the ground and their heads had been cut off, so that they had neither roots nor fronds — nothing but the stems. These were brought over, each in a long narrow deal box, in sawdust. When they arrived at Monserrate they were planted in large tubs of fine Serra, black mould and placed within the walls of the ruined chapel of 'Our Lady of Monserrate' and much care taken of them.

After a time they began to shoot out both roots and fronds, and when fairly established in vigour were transplanted to various parts of the grounds, where they grew apace, and are amongst the most beautiful objects at Monserrate. Of the first lot eight of the twelve succeeded.»

Cargill had been to Australia and is perhaps responsible for the striking resemblance that the Valley of the Tree Ferns, as it became known, bore to the forest glades of that country.

Enough of Cargill, what do we know of William Stockdale, the true genius of Francis Cook's garden?

Unfortunately very little. He was, to judge from his photograph (today in the collection of Branda, Lady Cook), an extraordinary character: a long white hairy beard and always a large black hat, he appears as an old man in the family photographs of the second viscount, Frederick. His paintings show him to have been a sensitive artist of the natural landscape, but there is nothing surviving that could be called a garden design. He had a house in South Brent on Exmoor in Devon.

By comparing iconography of different dates, as with the DeVisme/Beckford garden, we can surmise that much of the Romantic character of the present garden can be attributed to Stockdale. The earliest illustrations show crowded plantings in beds around the palace and scattered trees on the lawn that would have demonstrated the plant collections in a scientific manner. Earlier descriptions refer to «Dr. Cargill's Bed» a collection of flowering shrubs in a location where now exists the oldest group of exotic trees in the

The Chapel of Our Lady of Monserrate built by DeVisme and in ruins used as a garden ornament by Cook.

garden: a magnificent bosque that encloses the huge lawn and frames the view of the mountains from the palace. The scattered trees on the lawn were thinned to allow the most magnificent to develop.

By 1885, the gardens of Monserrate were famous. *The Gardeners' Chronicle*[82] (of London) published a long two-part article with a detailed description of the garden and an engraving. It is from this piece, by C.A.M. Carmichael, that we gain the clearest impression of Francis Cook's garden.

Mr. Cook who has travelled far and wide, unhesitatingly declares that his present home is the only place that ever tempted him to follow the pursuit of gardening outside England. He saw from the outset what the delight of it would be in such a temperature, how wide a scope for variety in vegetation he would have at his feet, and what the possibilities were, in such a position to a landscape gardener who was a child of nature not art.

Francis Cook, we are told, used to spend November, the greater part of April and June, and the whole of May on his Portuguese estate, during which time he took a great personal interest in the development of the garden. In particular the necessary thinning of the trees was given great attention. The early years had been spent in experiment, to discover what would grow; by 1885 Carmichael was able to write:

Palms and cycads are mingled with the singular vegetation of Mexico. Tree Ferns elbow Camellias, Ipomeas and Bougainvilleas cover entire walls and Tacsonias overpower tall trees in their rank luxuriance.[82]

What impressed him was seeing these plants growing freely, outdoors:

If the expression may be allowed for the nonce, the valley between the palacio and the dense slopes of the serra may well be called by English-tongues a vast open air greenhouse... Mr. Cook has been able to form in thirty years a garden which anyone ignorant of the rapidity of the vegetable growth in this climate would put down as the work of two life-times.[84]

The tower containing the Muses Room.

Gatehouse at Monserrate.

The «Roman Arch», Monserrate.

The Etruscan Fountain in Francis Cook's Garden.

A humorous kitchen sink, Monserrate.

Examples of this rapidity of growth are given, a *Thuja lobbii* described as «probably the best in Europe» is already eighty feet high (this is the prominent conifer at the foot of the palace that is so conspicuous in the early postcards — its growth allows us to date the photographs); Giant Araucarias on the lawn (which incidentally was «the only one in South Portugal» — the English must have their lawn!) are described as follows:

The best specimen of *Araucaria bidwillii* is 9 feet in girth at 1 foot and 7 feet 11 inches at four feet, the circumference of the branches is 60 yards and the height 65 feet. *A. Cunninghamii* is taller, but not so widespread, with a girth of 6 feet 5 inches at three feet. In the centre of the group are three Aexcelsas each approaching 80 feet in height; the middle one girths 8 feet 3 inches at three feet and the distance around the branches is 63 yards. [82]

Amazingly these trees were only twenty years old!

This article is important since it is written by a specialist and provides a list of the plants grown at that time. From it we can know that the principal provenances of these plants were Mexico, Australia, Brazil, Japan, China and South Africa. It also gives an idea of how these plants were used:

A great beauty... is formed by a tree which, having been blown across a path so as to leave ample passage has not been removed. An Actinidia was growing on the fallen tree. The climber continues to do so but being thrown near a tall *Grevillea robusta* 70 feet high, has also ascended it, and is flinging itself from branch to branch in wild luxuriance. The effect is indescribably beautiful, as other trees over run a similar manner by Tacsonias, Tecomas, and Maurandyas. [82]

Agave on the lawn at Monserrate at the turn of the century.

The second Visconde de Monserrate, Sir Frederick Cook, and his family at his Sintra property.

The garden was described by many visitors — the bibliography runs to some 100 items, many perhaps better written — but Carmichael has captured Francis Cook's dream «flinging itself from branch to branch in wild luxuriance», the effect *is* indescribably beautiful. The vine climbing the tall tree symbolises the Romantic paradise, a Jungle with which Sir Francis surrounded his Indian pavilions.

Sir Francis Cook, baronet, First Visconde de Monserrate, died in 1901 — the end of the Victorian age. His son Sir Frederick extended the dominion with the acquisition of Penha Verde, but the garden was brought to its peak of fame under the Third Visconde,

Sir Herbert Cook. Sir Herbert brought Walter Oates to Monserrate from La Mortola, the garden of Sir Thomas Hanbury where he had been head gardener, to develop the plant collections, in 1921. Walter Oates[83] in 1923 wrote a guide to the gardens — an indication of the number of visitors and the complexity of the gardens: at the same time more than 1000 species could be seen.

Pena and Monserrate quite definitely established the interest in, and the potential of, Sintra. The town was visited continually and suffered increasing pressure. Despite the fact that the access to Lisbon was considered one of the best, and according to Lichnowski

The Fonte da Pipa (Barrel Fountain), Sintra.

Views of the Old Town of Sintra taken from the same place in different centuries.

«perhaps the only road in Portugal», King Pedro V signed in 1855 a contract for the construction of a railway line to link it to the capital. Another 32 years were to pass, however, before the train actually reached Sintra. Meanwhile the site was chosen for the station and for future urban development which King Pedro V baptized with the name of his late wife, Estefânia.

Within the new spaces destined for housing, smaller buildings began to appear, almost carbon copies of European chalets but in cast-iron architecture following established patterns. During the first phase the decorations were executed in wooden cutouts, later with the spread of metallic elements, decorative details will be used in profusion.

Sintra possesses notable examples of Chalet architecture. Although not always to everyone's taste and if the truth be told, sometimes totally out of context, they do in their fantasy manage to capture a sense of «The Romantic Age» and of a more leisurely and serene era. Set into small lots of land, these houses generally have a tiny garden, in many of, which grows a giant Araucaria tree.

Vila Sassetti, Sintra. Following page, *the Chalet Biester, with the Moorish Castle in the background.*

Various views of the Chalet Biester.

Closer to the *Vila Velha* (the old town around the Royal Palace), other constructions were to be built towards the end of the nineteenth century which would enrich the artistic and monumental heritage of Sintra.

A curious example, as it is unique, is the «Villa» built by Carlos Sasseti, in Italianate style. Discreetly hidden among the trees, but enjoying the sunlight which floods the house, the *quattrocento* architecture is totally unexpected but incredibly it manages to blend with the extraordinary collection of exotic plants in the garden.

Chalet Biester, on the way to Pena, is in «a Queen Anne style which is in fact a *sui generis* romano-gothic combination!», the architect José Luís Monteiro, author of the project aimed:

only at an interpretation of that style and not its application. [84]

The park is well landscaped, particularly as regards the framing of its privileged views of the craggy peak of the Moorish castle.

At the end of the nineteenth century the last of the «great piles», fruit of an impassioned Romantic dream, was built: the new Quinta

Bow window over looking the gardens of Chalet Biester.
Above, *a view of the gardens.*

117

The exuberant neo-manueline architecture of the Quinta da Regaleira.

Garden of the Quinta da Regaleira.

da Regaleira commissioned by António Augusto Carvalho Monteiro.

The possessor of a large fortune, with a degree in law from Coimbra, this man began very early to dedicate himself to «collecting books, manuscripts, works of art» and curiosities. He owned the

largest collection of Camoes memorabilia in the world, consisting of thousands of literary works, manuscripts an sundry artistic objects, allusive to Camões. [85]

His interests, suggestive of the 16th century, led him to abandon the project of the landscape-architect Henry Lusseau, and express a preference for the fantastic neo-Manueline design by Manini, the set designer from the São Carlos Opera House. The land which Carvalho Monteiro had bought from Baron Regaleira was fed by many springs and was to be transformed into an extraordinary garden, laid out in a very specific programmed arrangement which told its own story.

Standing out like an enormous sculpture, the buildings of his Quinta exhibit a profusion of ornament in a copy of the more exuberant Manueline style. The detail of the sculpture is remarkable and shows the quality of the work of Portuguese artists at the end of the century. The materials of the interior finishings are very rich. This taste for quality and detail extends to the extraordinary iron gates made by local blacksmiths. In 1899, a local newspaper announced that the works were to begin shortly.

Quinta da Regaleira, the so-called «Wedding Cake»,
before the stone had weathered
— photographs taken soon after construction.

THE *CHALET* AND SOJOURNS IN SINTRA

THE arrival of the train in Sintra had made it more accessible. The «weekenders» had arrived, and families from the capital were frequent visitors.

The development of smaller plots of land, at prices within reach of these new visitors, had enabled them to build their weekend cottages in the Estefânia part of town, the Correnteza neighbourhood and then around the station and the casino. The model *par excellence* for these small houses was the chalet of which there are several versions.

But the great innovation of this century was brought about by Raul Lino, and represented a reaction against the proliferation of this style of architecture which was foreign to the local scenery. Raul Lino, devoted to Sintra and a lover and seeker out of the most hidden spots in the «serra», developed a new style of house. The studies he made of vernacular architecture in Portugal led him to produce a *grammar* of «the Portuguese house» for modern use.

As an artist he realized that the excessively sloped roofs of the chalets, resembling fir trees, were aggressive against such a pleasant landscape in which flourished the crowns of the umbrella pines:

Machine made or cast-iron ornamentation, multiplied until infinity and devoid of any of that charm without which there is no principle of beauty, should be banned from our houses and we should despise it for being useless and tedious.
There is at present amongst us the ungainly habit of placing the large prominent eaves on country houses, made in finished wood garnished with fragile curlicues in wood or cast-iron.
Nothing could be less appropriate.
For if we have lovely eaves in varied combinations all over the country, why should we not reproduce or develop them using new combinations? There are no lovelier eaves than those which are finished with the traditional Portuguese roof-tiles. The eaves on the so-called chalets would have been condemned a long time ago if we thought for one moment about their maintenance cost; they are rickety creations, and our climate is unforgiving: they can only be protected by layers of paint which are constantly renewed.
A good example of a wrong adaptation of a foreign construction process.[86]

Detail of a chalet, *Sintra.*

Chalets *in São Pedro de Sintra.*

The best example of Raul Lino's theories and of his works in Sintra is his own house in Sao Pedro, called Casa do Ciprestre. Raul Lino himself describes his house in these excellent words:

An old Ancestral Home, nonsense: we merely built a house which would be comfortable for its inhabitants and which, from the exterior, would be integrated in the beautiful Sintra landscape with sensitivity and respect.» [87]

The landscape, which had been forgotten by the chalet-owning bourgeoisie who came to Sintra merely to be fashionable, found a strong defendant in Raul Lino.

The model of the «Portuguese house» that he launched was widely adopted, such as at the Quinta de Santo António da Serra and Quinta Velha, or in urban developments of smaller size.

The advent of the car made it even easier to visit Sintra; with it came the day-trippers whose numbers increased annually. The spread of the capital and its suburban sprawl towards Sintra, place

House of the architect Raul Lino, in São Pedro de Sintra, known as the Casa do Cipreste (House of the Cypress).

it within even easier reach of the «Lisboetas». It is foreseeable that Sintra will increase its position, held for so long, as the privileged place of residence particularly now that the quality of the environment in urban areas has deteriorated to such an extent.

The 1980's have been marked by a return to the Quintas. They are being restored, although sometimes enthusiasm and haste have led to alterations which change the characteristics of the buildings irremediably.

An example of the spirit re-discovered by Raul Lino, which is the fruit of a continuity which modernism intended to put to an end, can be found in the delicate Quinta da Fonte Velha in Colares. Restoration of this Quinta began in 1972, and the gardens some ten years before. Dating back to the fifteenth century or earlier, the largely eighteenth century construction was altered by the unfortunate project of an architect who brought about its demise and finally its sale. The great attraction lay in the gardens on terraced slopes and avenues

Quinta Velha, Sintra,

Facing page,
*the view from the Belveder
at Quinta Velha.*

Small water tank at the Quinta da Fonte Velha.

Facing page, window at the Quinta da Fonte Velha, Colares.

A shaded walk at the Quinta da Fonte Velha.

In the gardens of the Quinta da Fonte Velha, a twenty-five year old Washingtonia palm.

with ancient boxwood, it had the melancholy flavour of abandon. The garden has been progressively restored and developed in harmony with the house, of which it intends to be but a continuation. The house in its turn relates to the garden in a tradition of noble rusticity. Today, within the Arcadian landscape of the valley, the Quinta da Fonte Velha presents a unified whole owing to a restoration which respected the character and message of a serene country family life.

The gardens in Italianate style would certainly have delighted its seventeenth century neighbour, the Bishop Dom Dinis de Melo e Castro. High box-hedges, fountains, belvederes with trellised lemon-trees, avenues of cypresses, all remind one of calm Florentine gardens. Its botanical collections recall how much Monserrate contributed to Sintra gardens.

Because this is a contemporary family residence which continues the traditions of life in Sintra, we believe that it is here that we should conclude this journey through the landscape and its Quintas.

For so long as one can find a caring hand unwilling to modernise what is so necessarily ancient, or to add novelties to disturb the religious and peaceful climate surrounding these Quintas... For as long as one can find in permanent residence a family with children and dogs... then Sintra will return all the love it has been given.

Facing page, a water tank in the gardens of the Quinta da Fonte Velha.

Gushing mask at the Quinta da Capela.

Much remains to be said, it may be asked why we have not dealt with this or that particular *Quinta*, but to end this work comes as a practicality and leaves many enchanting spots and noble gardens undescribed.

Sintra, just like its springs is eternally fresh, we have sought to illustrate this with those examples most pertinent to the historic and artistic progress that has been our method. We ask the reader therefore to forgive us for these omissions, and to remember that *Sintra* is also this: the charming villa that is encountered on the way, or even the childhood memory that is awakened by a twisted tree or massive rock. This enigmatic character of the Mountain has, we believe, been captured by the special ambience of the photographs; that character that makes *Sintra* once seen, never forgotten. The cult of the *Mons Sacro* will never lack devotees.

NOTES

[1] P. 9, Byron, *Letters and Journals of Lord Byron* (1898).

[2] P. 9, *Ibid*.

[3] P. 9, *Quintas*, this portuguese word that has been variously translated as farm or manor, or as we prefer villa, has been maintained along with certain others essential to all those interested in Sintriana. The word was often spelt «Kinta» by early English travellers which indicates how it should be pronounced. One other such word essential to the reader is *serra* the name given to the range of hills which is the backbone of Sintra. Incidentally the reader should note that modern spelling reform has rendered Byron's, CINTRA with an «s» making it easier to pronounce but removing the romantic connection of the name to the crescent moon of the town's history.

[4] P. 11, William Beckford, *Italy with Sketches of Spain and Portugal* p. 29 (1834).

[5] P. 11, *Ibid*, p. 28.

[6] P. 11, Robert Southey, *Letter to Samuel Taylor Coleridge*, April 1st (1800).

[7] P. 11, Beckford, *op. cit.*, July 9 th.

[8] P. 11, Genesis II, V.8.

[9] P. 11, Southey, *Journal*, April 30th (1800).

[10] P. 11, James Murphy, *Travels in Portugal*, p. 244 (1975).

[11] P. 11, Byron, v. ref. note 1.

[12] P. 11, Beckford, *Ibid*, p. 213.

[13] P. 11, Southey, *Letter*, October 7th (1800).

[14] P. 13, Beckford, *op. cit.*, p. 127.

[15] P. 13, Beckford, *op. cit.*, (Sea nymphs).

[16] P. 13, Eça de Queirós, *Os Maias*, Chapter VIII.

[17] P. 13, Beckford, *op. cit.*, p. 213.

[18] P. 15, Sachaverell Sitwell, *Portugal and Madeira*, p. 102 (1954).

[19] P. 15, Byron, *Childe Harold's Pilgrimage*, Canto IV, CLXXVIII.

[20] P. 15, Eça de Queirós, *Os Maias*, Chapter VII.

[21] P. 18, Borges Coelho, *Portugal na Espanha Árabe*, p. 65.

[22] P. 19, *Ibid.* text n.º 23, Vol. I, p. 85.

[23] P. 19, Sérgio Luís Carvalho, *A presença árabe em Sintra durante a Idade Média*, in *Historia n.º 101*, Lisboa, p. 92-93 (1987).

[24] P. 21, Santarém: fortress town in the Tagus Valley, North of Lisbon.

[25] P. 22, Francisco Costa, *O Paço Real de Sintra*, p. 33 (1980).

[26] P. 23, The House of Avis: second dynasty of Portuguese Kings founded by João at the Battle of Aljubarrota where he defeated the Castilian claim to the realm (1385).

[27] P. 27, Vítor Serrão, *Baixo-relevo tardo renascentista da Igreja Matriz de Rio de Mouro*, in *Sintria* I-II, p. 595 (1982-83).

[28] P. 27, *Sub tegmine fagi*, «under the shade of the beech trees», Virgil, *Eclogue* I.

[29] P. 27, *Otio fecundo*: literally means fertile leisure.

[30] P. 27, Rafael Moreira, *Francisco da Holanda* in *Sintria* I-II, p. 621 (1982-83).

[31] P. 28, *Ibid*.

[32] P. 28, Veríssimo Serrão, *História de Portugal*, Vol. III (1980).

[33] P. 29, Vítor Serrão, *opus cit.*, p. 588.

[34] P. 29, *Datur orae serenas*, «the gift of serene hours».

[35] P. 30, Reynaldo dos Santos, *A Escultura em Portugal*, Vol. III, p. 23 (1950).

[36] P. 30, Palace of Almeirim — near to Santarém, North of Lisbon.

[37] P. 30, Veríssimo Serrão, *op. cit.*, Vol. III.

[38] P. 30, An entailed estate. The Morgadio da Torre da Ribafria was first instituted in 1536 though the name was not used until 1541. «Torre» means tower.

[39] P. 32, *Solar*: Portuguese for Ancestral Home.

[40] P. 32, Severim de Faria, *Notícias de Portugal*, p. 85 (1740).

[41] P. 32, Carlos de Azevedo, *Solares Portugueses*.

[42] P. 34, «Town and Country Houses».

[43] P. 34, Vítor Serrão, *op. cit.*, p. 591.

[44] P. 35, António da Holanda: father Francisco da Holanda, the Portuguese painter author of *Diálogos em Roma* (1548) in which he records his conversations with Michelangelo.

[45] P. 35, António Vasconcelos Simão, *Os de Ribafria, Alcaides-Mores de Vila de Sintra* (1982).

[46] P. 35, Virgil, *Eclogue* VII, pp. 61-68. At the end of Virgil's eclogue Corydon says: The poplar pleases Hercules, the vine Bacchus, Myrtle for the beautiful Venus, for Apollo his Bay, Phyllis loves the Hazel, she loves it so that neither the myrtle of Venus, nor the Bay of Apollo exceed the hazel.
To which Thyrsis replies:
Ash is beautiful in the woods, Pine in the garden, Poplar by the riverside, Fir in the high mountains, but if fair Lycida would look on me once again what advantage would give the Ash in their woods and the Pine in their gardens.

[47] P. 38, A column with two arms or projections below the capital: this column is to be found on the ground floor supporting a small gallery.

[48] P. 39, In 1581, the Spanish King Philip II was crowned Philip I of Portugal inaugurating a 60 year period of Spanish domination.

[49] P. 40, Pedro Nunes (1502-78), mathematician and scientist, inventor of the *Nonius* an early micrometer.

[50] P. 40, Portuguese for «Hill of Recompense».

[51] P. 40, Horace, *Odes*.

[52] P. 40, Translations of Latin texts (Ref. *Velharias de Sintra I* by J.A. da Costa Azevedo).
João de Castro, who spent twenty years fighting for Christianity in the hardest of battles in the two Mauritanias, and who then not only traced the shores of Arabia and the coasts of all India, but also recorded them in his writings, on his return to his homeland, safe and sound, by the Grace of Christ, dedicated this chapel to the Virgin Mother (1542).

Go Forth Saved
Make Votive Promises
Go Forth Saved

Carry out the Promises
You will return saved
You will return saved.

[53] P. 40, Virgil.

[54] P. 41, Beckford *op. cit.*, p. 90.

[55] P. 41, L.B. Alberti, *Os Dez Livros da Arquitectura*, LVII, Chapter, IV.

[56] P. 41, Son of King Manuel I.

[57] P. 41, *Azulejos* — glazed tiles typical of Portuguese Art and Architecture.

[58] P. 43, Francisco Iniguez Almech, *Casas Reales y Jardines de Felipe II*, p. 49 (1952).

[59] P. 46, Ayres de Carvalho, *Dom João e a Arte no Seu Tempo* (1962).

[60] P. 49, Void.

[61] P. 54, Mardel — Hungarian Architect of Pombal's Palace de Oeiras.

[62] P. 57, William Beckford, *op. cit.*, p. 106-107. The favourite attendant was José Dias.

[63] P. 57, *Ibid.*, p. 105.

[64] P. 58, Oliveira Boleo, *Sintra e Seus Termos*, p. 32.

[65] P. 58, *Memoirs of William Hickey*, P. Quinnell Ed., p. 355 (1928).

[66] P. 60, Francisco Costa, *História da Quinta e Palácio de Monserrate* (1985).

[67] P. 66, Beckford, *Italy*...

[68] P. 64, Francisco Costa, *op. cit.*

[69] P. 64, Thomas of Erildonne (Thomas Cargill), *Fairy in Fairyland* (1870).

[70] P. 67, Visconde de Juromenha, *Cintra Pituresca*, 1828.

[71] P. 67, Christopher Thacker, *The History of Gardens*, p. 212 (1978).

[72] P. 69, Manuscript Anon. (1851), Biblioteca Municipal de Sintra.

[73] P. 72, Beckford, *op. cit.*, pp. 119-120.

[74] P. 73, William Elsden: English architect who worked in Coimbra and Oporto in the late eighteenth century.

[75] P. 74, These documents were brought to the attention of the town Library of Sintra where they are now to be found.

[76] P. 87, Inácio de Vilhena Barbosa, *Panorama Photographico de Portugal*, p. 10 (1873).

[77] P. 88, Rakzynski, *Les Arts en Portugal*.

[78] P. 94, José Teixeira, *Dom Fernando II: Rei Artista, Artista Rei*, p. 308 (1986). See also illustrations from Eugen Ruhl (1855) in this book.

[79] P. 103, Thomas of Ercildoune, *Fairylife in Fairyland* (1870), notes to part III.

[80] P. 103, Byron, *Childe Harold's Pilgrimage*, Canto I, XXIII.

[81] P. 106, Beckford, *op. cit.*, p. 220.

[82] P. 108, 110, *The Gardener's Chronicle*, September (1885).

[83] P. 112, W. Oates, *A Pequena Guia*, Monserrate (1923).

[84] P. 117, *A Architectura Portuguesa*, April (1908).

[85] P. 121, Mimosa Barreto, «Carvalho Monteiro, Mecenas da Cultura», in *Cadernos de Museologia*. APOM, colóquio APOM-83-Actas, pp. 44-46 (1986).

[86] P. 123, Raul Lino, *A Nossa Casa*, 3rd edition, p. 40.

[87] P. 124, Raul Lino, *Exposição Retrospectiva da Sua Obra*, Catalogue Fundação Calouste Gulbenkian, p. 12 (1970).

The fifth
edition
was printed
in March of 2000.
The text is composed
in 10/11 point souvenir light
the paper used
was 150 g. Inagloss
The normal edition has been produced
with 1000 examples in Portuguese
and 1000 in English

Odruhas

Toueira

S. João das Lampedas

Magoute

Bolembra

Montelavar

Conselho

Junqueira

Chilreira

Codaceira

Pernige

S. João do Torrage

Morcle

Fontanellas

Aldea Gallega

Gouvea

Villa Verde

S. Mamede

Meirones

Q.ª Granzea

M.ºˢ da Torre

Condado

Camporeso

Jeina

Corigoz

Mourelinho

Collares

Navarros

Carrascal

Cabrux

Granja do Marquez

Q.ª da Madre de Deos

Varzea

Q.ª de Varzea

Q.ª do Cigu.

Loural

Algerão

COLLARES

S. Bento

Q.ª do Vinagre

Bemposta

Q.ª de Monserrate

CINTRA

Almoçageme

Penha Verde

Q.ª de Rio de Milho

Val de Parra

Melessa

Penedo

Convento dos Capuchos

Ch.ᵉ de Maias

S. Pedro

Cazas Novas

Q.ª do Ramalhão

Chafariz

Olgeira

Cruz da meia

Charneca

Covas

Atalaia

Abrunheira

Azoya

F.ᵗᵉ da Roca

Penha

Linhó

Moncôrvo

Biscaia

V.ª do Monte

Ranholos

Aloandraque

Fontainha

Q.ª do Mercador

Capa-rota

Cabrafica

Fran

Almoinhas Velhas

Zambujal

Q.ª de S. Martinho

Manique

de Cima

Malveira

Adruana

Peneda

Torzela

M.ᵗᵉ do Alcoutão

F. do Guincho

Q.ª de Angeja

Carrascal

Trajouce

Alcoutão

Polima

Murtaes

Alcabideque

V.ª das Neves

Miradouro

Cazaes

Vicece

Onteiro

Cabreiras

Bat.ʳⁱᵃ da Galle

Bocharda

Puygordo

Tires

Bat.ᵗⁱᵃ Alauté

Area

Birre

Alvito

Meragata

V.ᵗᵉ da Crespina

Cobres

Lugar da Torre

Estoril

Caliza

Lapraia

Zambujal

F. de S. Braz da Sinchete

S.ᵗᵒ Antonio

Penedo

S. Domingos

F. de S. Jorge

CASCAES

Murtal

Phare da Guia

F. de S.ᵗᵒ Antonio

Rana

Paredes

Saqueiro

F. da Guia

Citadelle

OEIRAS

Revelim

Carcavelos